Praise for *Se...*

"When Kirsten Reneau takes us to the extremes of experience, she points at what someone else might consider trivial (a cicada, bar bathroom graffiti, a coffee filter), transforming observation into insight. *Sensitive Creatures* is an incredible accomplishment. I'm already excited to reread it."

—Jeannie Vanasco, author of *Things We Didn't Talk About When I Was a Girl* and winner of the Ohioana Book Award

"*Sensitive Creatures* is an emotional journey, taking readers through personal experiences where nothing is held back and the experiences of humanity are poetically bound to the animal world. Kirsten Reneau's essays are captivating, standing vigil over the past and showing readers how the world can be cruel, or beautiful, or often both."

—Leah Myers, author of *Thinning Blood: A Memoir of Family, Myth, and Identity*

"Reneau's beautiful, at times harrowing, debut collection of essays draws insights from nature as it chronicles her coming of age in a world that feels teeming with both danger and wonder. With poetic vigilance and formal experimentation, these essays are by turns playful and devastating. Yes, these pages hold their fair share of pain and grief but ultimately, like her cicadas and newts and hummingbirds, Reneau's writing finds sustaining connection in the world—both grounded and exhilarating."

—Anne Gisleson, author of *The Futilitarians*

SENSITIVE CREATURES

SENSITIVE CREATURES

ESSAYS

KIRSTEN RENEAU

Fort Smith, Arkansas

SENSITIVE CREATURES

© 2024 by Kirsten Reneau
All rights reserved

Cover image: John Gould, *Phaethornis Griseogularis, ca. 1850*
(Detroit Institute of Arts). Digitally enhanced via rawpixel.

Newt: from *The Naturalist's Miscellany* (1789–1813) by George Shaw
Scorpius: via Canva Pro License

Edited by Casie Dodd
Design & typography by Belle Point Press

Belle Point Press, LLC
Fort Smith, Arkansas
bellepointpress.com
editor@bellepointpress.com

Find Belle Point Press
on Facebook, Substack,
and Instagram (@bellepointpress)

Printed in the United States of America

28 27 26 25 24   1 2 3 4 5

Library of Congress Control Number: 2024931653

ISBN: 978-1-960215-13-0

SC/BPP25

A Note

The following work is based on true events, or as true as I can remember them to be. Because they are based on a real, lived life, and because life is not always easy, there are descriptions—sometimes graphic and explicit, sometimes not—of sexual assault, rape, disordered eating, and other violences. But much like life, there are beautiful things—descriptions of falling in love and very good coffee, for example—here too.

CONTENTS

To West Virginia,
to New Orleans,
to the people and animals
who enabled me to survive in both places,
and always, to Alex.

A Prologue

THE FIRST THING you must know is this: several kinds of newts can regenerate their entire body in pieces. The limbs, the eyes, the spinal cord, the brain, the heart—as long as these are taken from them individually, plucked and pulled from the body one at a time, they can regrow them shiny and new, and the newt continues living.

The newt recreates its broken pieces with fresh tissue. This tissue is a technically perfect biological match for the body it left behind. However, in some small way, there will be an imperfection, a difference between what it lost and what it gained. This is the marker that this is not its original form; there is something fundamentally different about them.

The second thing you must know is this: it is amazingly easy for a person to lose a piece of themselves by accident, become split into two uneven parts. Considering the trauma of it all, you would think it would be harder.

Most animals (humans, for example) heal their physical wounds with scar tissue, hardened markers of where the hurt was. This tells us that the healing process, despite its importance, may be ugly. Sometimes my thumb rolls over the scars on my skin: a long white line across my pointer finger from a set of scissors; a pale dash from a mattress spring that is as white as the day it first scarred over; dots from bug bites half-healed and pulled off over and over again. I am known for picking at open wounds.

Emotional hurt is different. Scientists believe that humans' DNA can carry memories of traumatic stress, changing a person on a molecular level. Eventually, the body may be sewn back together, but there will always be something fundamentally different, and we carry that for the rest of our lives.

PART ONE: THE WRECKAGE WE DO

WHAT I REMEMBER

REMEMBER useless things, facts that never offer anyone anything. How a giraffe's heart weighs twenty-five pounds; that a fire chaser beetle spends its entire life looking for flames; that there are two kinds of lightning—positive and negative. How lightning always comes before thunder—that is, the crash, the sound of a thousand plates breaking, must come after the light.

I remember wanting, how my first want was to live in the same way humans first wanted to create fire—an evolutionary desire grown from the millions of ancestors that had all survived long enough to offer another generation. I remember how I grew to feel want in my body. How it made me hot to the touch. How it felt when I was wanted, how I was certain he would scorch his fingertips off when he entered them inside me. How I felt like the blue center of a fire.

I remember the snow when I was young, the way it made the earth feel quiet and reverent. How going outside felt like going into church. How I once fell and cut my finger open on a ski and after, I sat by the fireplace, watching the flames eat. How I learned fire on a wound can close it off. How later, I went out in the snow in T-shirts, in shorts, how it would turn my nose runny and red, and I would be sick for days after. How I wanted to be sick, then, in a way that people could see, so that it could be real.

I remember how he made me feel sick, then, but no one could see it. How it felt like my insides were turning black and burnt, like the fire in my body was charring my lungs. How I woke up coughing from the chest. I remember his hand over my shirt, under it, skin on skin, the heat of his palm. How I thought I was going to be branded with the imprint of his fingertips on my breast. How I wanted to cry when I found bruises after waking up on his mattress the next morning. I remember the blood between my legs for days after.

I remember all the times I wanted to die after the same way I remember all the times I fell asleep. How it has really all become one collective moment of memory, drawn from the shared pool of memories. How I once saw a thunder snowstorm, watched lightning strike between falling snowflakes. How ridiculous it seemed, that these two things could exist at the same time. How ridiculous it is that I sometimes feel like glass, like shattered fragments of two different people.

I remember useless things: how a fire chaser beetle searches for flames so she can eat the burnt bark of a tree turned dead. How she cannot smell the smoke but, rather, feels for the heat. I remember how lightning always comes before thunder—that is, the crash must come after the crackling light, blinding, able to burn entire cities to the ground. I remember how it feels to burn.

DID DOLPHINS CRY?

THE FIRST TIME I had sex, I expected that I would, at the very lewast, cry. It's easy to make me cry, really—I weep at feel-good stories on the radio, and I once had to blink back tears after reading the Wikipedia article for *Sophie's Choice*. Happy movies, sad books, thinking about my dog too hard—really anything can make me shed a few emotional tears.

With that in mind, I thought it stood to reason that I would get emotional after my boyfriend and I stumbled our way through what I thought was the ultimate cumulation of true intimacy for the first time. After all, M was my first real boyfriend and we were in love, so it stood to reason that everything would go perfectly. He had been asking and I had been putting it off and now, several months into our romance, it seemed like it was time to give in. If not now, when? If not him, who?

Sure, there had been other short flings with men who had attempted to push their hands down my pants on bus rides or searched for my bra clasp sitting behind me in history class. I understood that they were to be treated like mosquitos: an annoyance but part of life. I learned that men were always going to be asking, and that it was my job to say no repeatedly, and that this was the cycle we would do until I was not attractive anymore—which, as I understood in high school, was going to be around the age of twenty-five.

So I had a hidden fear that, since M was the first person that had shown active interest in not only having sex with me but also committing himself to me, he would also be the last. Sex with me was a reward I would be giving him for his persistence and kindness.

And M was truly kind. He lived in the next county over and would drive an hour across the mountains each way to see me every weekend. He tutored me in math. I took him to the homecoming dance and there, we danced, and he kissed my ear and told me he loved me over and over again. These signals of devotion, I was sure, meant we would be together forever, or at least a while.

I knew that Jamie, who sat next to me in Health Class during our freshman year of high school, had cried. It was in the same class that someone had etched a dolphin into my desk years before. I traced the grooves that had been carved into the wood as my teacher stuck pieces of scotch tape on us and told everyone that it was like having sex; *you know, the first time, it sticks. Emotionally, that is.* Then she would take the same piece of tape and put it on someone else and point out how it had lost its stickiness and couldn't bond to the new person, *and that, kids, is why you should wait until marriage.*

Jamie cried because it physically hurt, she said—the literal act. But I didn't expect to cry because of pain. My parents, always willing to avoid awkward conversations and unexpected pregnancies, gave me a book about having safe sex, and I came to my boyfriend ready with condoms and lube that I vaguely understood how to use.

But my other friend, she said that she cried because she got so emotional, and she and her boyfriend just held each other for a long, long time after, and I thought maybe I would cry like that. Like maybe it would be an opening, an awakening in myself, or between me and M, who I just knew that I loved so much—that we would both (or at least, I) be so overcome with emotion by this beautiful thing we had done together that it would bring me to just a few soft tears, which he would gently wipe away in the afterglow, a story we would fondly recall after we were married—and somehow both rich and happy too.

What really happened was that while *Friends* played in the background and snow fell softly outside my parents' home, he lingered over me on the too-small basement couch, and it worked for maybe all of three minutes before I told him, *I'm sorry, but please get out of me; it hurts*. And he waited another minute before he did, and for this, I forgave him instantly, because what else could I have done?

Because he was kind for a teenage boy (who are not always known for their amazing empathy), he apologized over and over again while he pulled up his pants and kissed my shoulders, and I didn't shed one single tear, much less feel any kind of awakening or a connection.

As I put my shirt back on, I thought of how I once read on some online listicle that dolphins were the only animals other than humans that had sex for pleasure and wondered if it hurt for them too, if teenage dolphins had to hide from their parents, if they worried about birth control or unexpected pregnancies or the emotional repercussions of sex too early. Did dolphins cry?

"What are you thinking about?" M asked me as he buckled his jeans.

"Nothing," I said, not wanting to admit that after losing my virginity I could only think about dolphins.

"How does it feel, not being a virgin?" he asked.

I knew I was supposed to feel something, some kind of way about myself, but it was like a birthday party where people keep asking you how old you are, and you keep saying the wrong age because nothing actually feels different.

The next morning, I slept in while my family went to church. When I woke up, I watched *Out of Africa* alone in the house, and Meryl Streep was so beautiful that I cried.

AN INCREDIBLY BRIEF AND UNFINISHED HISTORY OF SOUND

1.

They don't think that the Big Bang was much like a bang at all. It was a rumbling bass that first shook the universe so hard that galaxies seeped out of nothingness, dripping dark matter and future life. Had one existed, no human ear would have been able to hear it.

The scientist who discovered this recreated the noise, the release of nothingness into everythingness, when he got a letter from an 11-year-old who was working on a school project. This scientist used a NASA satellite, plugging in the frequency spectrum, and immediately his two dogs ran into the room, howling in a way that only animals who know something can. He had to transcribe it up several decimals before he, too, could hear what made his dogs cry.

When I first heard the noise, played for me by a boy who made me want to touch the stars, I forgot how to breathe. M was my first real boyfriend and I sat in his room—one of his hands on my thigh, the other on his computer mouse—both of us acutely aware his mother could walk in at any moment.

Everyone knows the sound of a dropping bomb, shown to us in cartoons and history documentaries alike. It is the slow build-up before the great explosion, an anxiety-inducing drop of a whistle. It is every ugly bomb that has ever dropped and each single droplet that has disrupted the quiet of still water. All fear, all tension, all build-up.

And that was the first sound.

2.

We have to talk. It always starts like that, doesn't it? Or maybe sometimes they get creative, and it's *I need to tell you something.*

That's where bad news always begins, rooted against the back of our jaws. It's no easier to be the messenger sometimes, and the language can taste thick against the roof of your mouth, coating the tongue heavy and dense. But it's not the words that we are afraid of saying. It is what follows—the quiet.

3.

I close my eyes and inhale deeply, breathing in the air that lies heavy around me. The air is different here, and I know that—it is drenched in humidity from the water that threatens to break the shoreline in half. I am thousands of miles away from home, from West Virginia, from the fresh air of the mountains. The wind carries the faint scent of smoke, like the pipes my grandfather used to light. Now the tobacco takes the form of cigarettes, and they are mine.

A stranger on the street once called them coffin nails, and I liked that so much that I gave him one. These things make it harder to fill my lungs completely, but I do it anyway—I breathe deeply, and my chest rises.

From the air in the chest, small puffs vibrate up the throat, sifting their way against a muscle just about the size of the walnuts I used to pluck from trees in my backyard. In men, you can watch the larynx move up and down like a fishing bob, delicately finding its balance on their necks.

Finally, stretched tightly across the top of the throat are the vocal cords. They are two folds of mucous membrane, all pink and softness, cut like a slit (|). It is a reminder that we all began as women. The vocal cords do vibrate but not in the way that my sixth-grade science class taught me. The human form is far more delicate than that.

The total surface area of the cords that vibrate is no bigger than half of my very smallest fingernail. What a powerful muscle, this minuscule section of our body responsible for expressing some of our greatest joys and heartbreaks.

I exhale outwards again.

4.

The ocean is more expansive than we can wrap our brains around, and somewhere in the Pacific there is a pod of whales that are swimming together. They talk to each other without grammar and syntax but in a series of clicks, whistles, and pulsed calls.

The clicks help with navigation. Bouncing off objects, the noise will seamlessly return to the whale, and slowly it will be able to make out the shape of what is coming. Whistles and pulsed calls are for socializing. They help differentiate between friend and not-yet friend. Whales are very much human in how we both love to be with each other, in our desire to be known.

But there is a whale that is different. It is either a fin whale or a blue whale, or perhaps it is a combination of the two, a strange but not unheard-of hybrid that must balance itself somewhere in between. He is male, and he calls during mating season the way that male whales do. He was first recorded in 1989, still profoundly deep to the human ear but about fifteen hertz above average for a whale. The scientists picked up the same mating call time and time again, and for twelve years this whale cried in such a way that scientists had never heard before.

So the question came: Could anyone hear him?

5.

I have something to tell you. It is not a threat or even a promise of impending gossip to be whispered about at high school the next day. It is a declaration, and I know that without words but by the way he looks at me in the mid-October heat, our teenage bodies golden against the falling sun. Around us, the leaves have begun to change color. The mountains around look like an oil painting come to life.

I am in love with you, M says. *And it's really okay if you don't feel the same way, but I just wanted to let you know that this is how I feel, and you know that you don't have to say it back but I just really wanted you to know—*

I do not say anything. I wrap my arms around his body and press my forehead to his shoulder. The Adam's apple stops moving. He pulls me closer, and we rest in the quiet.

6.

Om! This syllable is the whole world, the Mandukya Upanishad begins. It is the states of time, the states of consciousness, and all of knowledge— the primordial sound of the universe. In meditation, it becomes almost a hum that shakes both the individual cells of the body and the reverberation against the cosmos, and that tiny muscle in our throats swells to the occasion.

The physical world falls into the background, and this single syllable comes into its power.

One Sanskrit document suggests that our body, in its perishable state of being, is the first fuel stick, and Om is the second. With discipline and diligence, the rubbing together of these sticks will start a fire full of thoughts and self-awareness that bursts from one's self. The text claims that Om is a tool of empowerment, to allow one to know the god that sits inside of ourselves, nestled in the chest, right where language itself (and thus, the world) begins.

7.

The whale.

He would have left his mother at around six or seven months but wouldn't have reached maturity until he was twenty-five years old. Normally, they would live in groups of six to ten, traveling up and down the expansive nothingness and everythingness that the water has to offer. Because of the enormous size of the blue whale, it has no natural predators other than the occasional orca.

Maybe he was attacked once and bears the scars across his tail—white, angry chalk lines cutting against the fin. Maybe this was the first time he had been touched since he left his mother.

Fin whales can live for 140 years; blue whales have not been studied enough to have a clear tell of just how long their lives can stretch. When no one can hear you, it may feel as long as the ocean itself. Because he has no predators, the whale is doomed to live until he simply cannot anymore, calling to a void year after year and hearing nothing in return.

Does he know?

Could a whale understand the echoing silence that is loneliness?

8.

We learn to cry before we learn to speak.

Like the whales, we too learn to communicate without linguistic structure, but rather, three different types of crying. The first of these is the basic cry, which follows a systematic pattern of crying and silence, crying and silence, and sometimes, with an inspiratory whistle. Next is the angry cry; while this sounds similar in pattern to the normal cry, it is stronger, louder, more likely to hurt. The third is the pain cry, which is often one long scream, followed by a period of holding one's breath.

As babies, we cry because everything is the first time—we believe hunger could kill us, so we cry. We believe the stuffed animal could kill us, so we cry. We believe the person we love more than anything in the world leaving could kill us, so we cry. Some of these things, we never outgrow.

My mother says I cried the most when she left me. I would scream for her when she wasn't within eyesight, more than either of my sisters. I cried often as a child—I cry often now. But growing up, it was closer to wailing, a half scream half sob that left me with full red cheeks and a scratchy voice.

In those times, my parents often left me alone. There was nothing they could do. I would weep until I had worn myself out, until the only sounds were just me heaving, punctuating the stale air with sharp breaths inward. And then it would be quiet again.

The Greek poet Sappho once wrote, "What cannot be said will be wept."

In that case, I wonder how many unspoken words are behind an ocean made of saltwater tears.

9.

M eventually broke up with me. I loved him too, but there was a loneliness that sat inside of my chest, filling up the empty space between air and the inner god I could not find, and it did not leave me, despite all his declarations. Call it miscommunication.

He told me in his car, *Listen, we have to talk* . . . But there was very little "we" in terms of talking. After he was done speaking and I was done listening, we sat in silence, an unbearable weight between us, pressing against the divot of my throat; I thought I would die if I had to spend one more minute in the suffocating pressure that had crept into the air around us, dense with the pain of knowing I was unwanted. Nothing felt so empty and so large as the space that hung in that silence.

10.

When people learned about the whale, the scientists who discovered him started getting letters. Some asked how they could help the whale find others, draw him out of isolation and teach him to communicate. Some realized that the story of this creature they would never know broke something inside of them, because they too were not being heard. It was mostly women who wrote to them.

After twelve years, they no longer were able to follow the whale's path. The last interview on the matter was given in 2012. Since then, there have been songs, sculptures, films, and even a short-lived Twitter account dedicated to what had been dubbed "The World's Loneliest Whale."

But here's the tic—the whale speaks differently, but they are unsure if that really means anything at all, other than a minor vocal abnormality. If you talk to the scientists, they don't know if other whales can or cannot hear him—which means they could, which means the question is not about the whale anymore, but instead it is about the people: why do we want the whale to be lonely?

11.

It was August 1952 when John Cage first presented the three-movement composition 4'33". This was at the regal Maverick Concert Hall in New York as part of a recital focused on contemporary piano music. The pianist came out, sat down at the bench, and, to mark the beginning of the piece, closed the lid. He later opened it briefly to mark the end of the first movement—and again for the second and third.

When asked about the composition, Cage said, "They missed the point."

"There's no such thing as silence. What they thought was silence, because they didn't know how to listen, was full of accidental sounds. You could hear the wind stirring outside during the first movement. During the second, raindrops began pattering the roof, and during the third the people themselves made all kinds of interesting sounds as they talked or walked out."

Some have called it "four minutes, thirty-three seconds of silence," but that's not quite right. It is four minutes, thirty-three seconds of humanity, of strangers listening to the nothingness and everythingness that the universe has to offer.

12.

After that car ride, I spent four days alone in my room.

The air was heavy then too. I did not shower. I barely ate. When I finally emerged, hair soaked by the build-up of humidity, my body tired in its loneliness, I went to my friend and I told him about how much it hurt. I didn't know what I needed except company.

Being a good friend, he picked me up from my house and we drove to a field nearby. He let me talk, and when I was done, he did not try to give me an uplifting speech or a motivational sermon.

He said, *I hear you.*

In the quietness that followed, we listened as the crickets began to sing.

HOW THE CICADA SCREAMS

ONCE accidentally dug up a cicada in the springtime, killing it right before it was meant to fly. The house I lived in, my parents' house, had a ring of plants around it—the man who lived there before, by most accounts a generally grumpy and not well-liked neighbor, had been an expert gardener, and he tended to all sorts of flowers and bushes that made our yard lush and attractive in ways we could not.

No one in my family ever knew much of anything about gardening. But every now and then one of us would get the notion to try to plant some tulips, and that might have been why I was digging the day I unearthed the cicada. Most of that week is only memory in passing, threads I am barely able to hold onto, but I remember his body under the butterfly bush, which stood large with lilac flowers.

It must have been only a few months, maybe even just a few weeks, before he was supposed to wake up. The cicada, that is. The swarm had last been seen in the nineties, and every year the farmers that congregated by the Church of the Nazarene suspected that this was finally the year the plague would turn upon our houses. Most years they were wrong, but this time they were finally right. All spring, there was a sense of Old Testament doom hanging in the air, making it hard to breathe.

The periodical cicadas (*magicicada*) will burrow into the hollow of the ground, create a home inside the dirt, and live there for thirteen or seventeen years, depending on the brood type. They do not see the sun, instead spending most of their life resting, growing, preparing. After over a decade of gestating inside the earth, they will emerge, spend a week shedding the hard outer layer of skin, and then scream their way across the countryside. I've always found it kind of admirable, to be able to express yourself so freely like that.

While there are annual cicadas, those that come up every year, the periodical cicadas, like he was, are perfectly developmentally synchronized—they emerge as adults together, either on the thirteenth or seventeenth year. It is a prime number, always, which works as a defense mechanism; it makes it harder for other animals to biologically sync up their own schedules to the cicada appearances. As a nymph, he would live just around two feet under the surface, drinking the juice of deciduous trees.

They eventually emerge on a spring evening. The perfect synchronization coded into their DNA means they all work under very exact conditions, coming out only when the soil temperature at eight inches deep is greater than sixty-four degrees Fahrenheit. He would have been born from the earth in late May and molted one more time, spending six days hiding in the trees, waiting for his exoskeletons to harden. After that, he would have started singing.

Mythology tells us that Eos, the goddess of dawn, was cursed by Aphrodite to be perpetually in love and in lust, which led her to take on a string of mortal lovers. This included a Trojan prince named Tithonus. A vase shows Eos chasing after him, and Tithonus holds a lyre, reluctant to be caught. Sappho recorded their story, which almost doubles as a warning.

Eos, so obsessed with her mortal companion, asked Zeus to turn him immortal so they could spend the rest of eternity welcoming mornings together. There is no information on whether Tithonus was consulted.

Zeus granted Eos's wish, but the goddess forgot to ask for eternal youth. While Tithonus did not die, he did age, until his skin became loose and heavy, and his spine curled into a circle. He outlived his eyes and tongue, no longer able to see, no longer able to talk. He lived for a hundred lifetimes, growing so small, so shriveled, that he became the world's first cicada.

The week I killed the cicada, I was on spring break. I was in college and had no interest in staying with my parents for the entire week off. For the first couple of days, I went to stay with a friend in the city nearby. I was young enough and came from a town small enough that going out to bars was still an event. We'd sleep all day and emerge at night to meet up with strangers, tall men with biblical-sounding names and deep voices. One time, one of them bought me shots of Crown Royal and drove us home. While my friend was throwing up in the bathroom, he pushed me over the kitchen table, making my body curve like a tree that can't stand on its own. I don't remember his name. I don't remember the color of his hair. I remember the taste of whiskey as I bit my tongue and tried not to throw up too. I stared at the tiles, the black-and-white checkered pattern, trying to imagine the floor below us, and then the earth below that, the dirt below dirt, imagining I was there, nestled in the dark soft ground, anywhere that wasn't under the too-bright fluorescent lights of the kitchen.

A fact: There is a reason cicadas stay buried for so long. It makes them harder to kill. Due to the extra-long time they spend below ground, they are unreliable prey for any predator that wants to eat regularly. Though they're vulnerable in their first week above earth, as they molt and adjust to their new bodies, their new lives, the sheer number of them emerging all at once helps ensure that most of the individuals make it through that first week. The reason behind everything the cicada does comes down to the core strand woven into their DNA: an unshakable desire to survive.

Another fact: The cicada has no defenses. It cannot sting, it doesn't normally bite, and it is not venomous. The cicada, on its own, is as fragile as the single petal of a flower. This seems to be at odds with their survival instinct.

I did end up throwing up in that kitchen. After he ejaculated and left, I emptied my stomach until my throat felt exposed, as if it had been skinned. I fell asleep on the couch. My friend and I laughed about it the next morning because I didn't want it to be a big deal; I didn't want to be the one who made it a big deal—it couldn't be a big deal if we were laughing.

God, we were so drunk. We laughed because it was just so funny. *I can't believe I threw up in the sink.*

I went home that day and slept long and hard. The next afternoon (or was it morning?) I was digging into the soft dirt and found the cicada. He was impossibly small, a curled comma, the skin dark and hard, his arms splayed outwards as if he was in the middle of digging. Holding it in my palms, my chest felt open and hollow. It had never been able to breathe open air, but it was so close. The guilt settled in my stomach, turning vile and rotten.

Who was I to rip it from the earth?
Who was I to turn his home into a grave?
Why me?
What had I done wrong?
What was wrong with me?

When I left for school again, I began wearing oversized sweatshirts, creating an exoskeleton of my own, and started dreaming of being buried alive, forced to swallow dirt. I often woke up coughing deeply, from the chest.

Cicadas are littered through folklore and mythology, featured in songs, literature, art, and food. For as long as they've existed, they have been consumed and digested for their healing properties. Their rarity offers them power, and the cicada molt is sweet and cold and, in Chinese folklore, is thought to help with fevers, issues of the eyes, and sore throats that feel as if they had been scratched raw.

When I came home that summer, I stopped leaving my room when I didn't have to. I slept often, curled up under layers of thick, dark blankets. I worked at a children's camp where I had to sing five days a week, for five weeks straight—the entire month of June and first week of July. I often dreamt of men who would pull my bones out of my body, leaving me loose and alone. Everything always seemed heavy. The butterfly bush stopped flowering.

What is happening to you? My mother asked me once.

I shrugged. I didn't talk much when I didn't have to.

The singing of male cicadas is produced not from the throat, but rather from the chest. They use a pair of tymbals, sound-producing organs attached to their abdominal regions, which rapidly relax and then tense, over and over again, making their mating call. Depending on their position, they can modulate the song or amplify it. In some species, a single male cicada can call as loud as thunder. It is enough to cause permanent hearing loss in most people, if they're close enough.

Periodical cicadas will sing for twenty-four hours straight on the hottest days of the summer, in a chorus together. The pitch feels continuous to the human ear, and it is nearly impossible for the average person to find where in the trees the cicada may be hiding in plain sight. It almost becomes like static.

How did Tithonus feel when he realized what his life was to become? What was it like to curl into his own body—lie in the dirt so long that it became a blanket—and become new again? He was not given the ability to speak to his former lover but was offered the power to scream instead. Is that what he wanted to do anyway?

In most mythology, the cicadas represent rebirth and immortality. The Aztecs carved the insect from jade and used it in funeral rituals, placing it on the tongues of the dead. Even its genus name, *Magicicada,* comes from the Greek word *magi,* or magic.

As the summer wore on, I still had the dreams. I began going outside at night, driving into the forest, hiding among tall deciduous trees that were green and alive. Always, the cicadas spoke. I tried to make myself familiar with their language, as if they could offer me a secret I needed. I whispered promises into the trees. I apologized over and over and over again. Once I screamed back. I was so loud that the dogs nearby began howling, too. Then we were all just making noise, a symphony of animals trying to be heard, trying to bait the universe into giving answers to a question I didn't know how to ask.

Unlike the butterfly or moth, the cicada has no pupal state. Rather, it is one single moment of change that sets them up for the unbearable weight of being alive.

The cicadas more or less die out by mid-July. Once they emerge, they only live for a few weeks—they mate, plant eggs, and as they die, the next generation begins to grow underground. They survive.

ONCE, I SAW A MONARCH BUTTERFLY DEAD ON THE PAVEMENT—

BROWN AND BLACK wings folded, one over the other, as if it was sleeping, curled into the fetal position. It was Sunday morning, and people were leaving the church I sometimes pretended I went to. I was hoping that the bundles of people walking by the white cross, clutching their programs, wouldn't notice that my clothes smelled of gin and weed. I was so rarely alone then, always needing to be surrounded by others in order to not be myself, but I was walking home from a one-night stand from a man who I never wanted to see again. He wasn't bad, just some guy in a string of some guys that I didn't care about and that didn't care about me. I felt like throwing up. I felt like going back, just so I wouldn't have to be alone and face an unnamable feeling of guilt that followed me like a bad dream. It was cold outside, the bitter cold of a knife's edge. I remember because I was wearing shorts, because the night before I was drunk and had tripped on concrete and tore my skin up as we crossed the bridge. I was shaking as I tried to walk, my skin pricked up at the wind that threatened to cut through me to the bone. For a minute I thought maybe that's why the monarch was dead, that the cold bit right through it, but then a car drove by and over the busted wing, and I realized the truth. There is no patron saint for butterflies that land in the middle of the road, but maybe it's for the best. There's no beauty in it, to be the saint of something that thought maybe they were born destined for destruction.

To Survive Hypothermia, You Must Ignore Everything Your Body Tells You

AFTER, when I was drunk, I told Nick that I thought I lived in a constant state of crisis. We were drinking, and I was drunk because I was always drinking and drunk then, making my body a Molotov cocktail to be thrown at whoever would catch it, open-palmed. I quickly learned that Nick was not afraid of burning, from fire or frostbite.

We had known each other for a day, maybe two by then, an intense weekend in the middle of the coldest winter I could remember. During the day, we drove up a road layered in white ice and hiked across snow at least six inches high, our footprints as light as birds. In the night our arms and legs and eyes became a tangle of tree branches, kindling for a fire that burned out as quickly as it started. So we were out again, drinking. We didn't know each other, but thought we did, and that made us more honest.

He asked me to explain myself, his thumb rolling over my knee, feeling for my skin in the dark of the bar. I couldn't. It was innate—a violence embedded within me, by me, against me. I knew the words were true in the same way I know the shape of the scar on my left pointer finger, cut by a pair of scissors over a piano when I was ten.

He shrugged. He was a lapsed Catholic. He knew all about crisis; he was in one himself. It's why we were drawn together, to the wild pieces of the other. Chaos loves company. We drank more. When we left the bar, the snow was still falling and the wind so strong that all I could see was the bright light of nothing. I walked forward anyways, the outline of my body fading away before he could leave me behind.

QUIZ:
DO YOU HAVE A HEALTHY
RELATIONSHIP TO SEX?

WE ALL KNOW that sex is made up of more than just the physical act. There's your relationship to your body, your relationship to others, your feelings of self-worth, and so much more. Sex is a core, basic human need to many, and the complications of these intersections can be endless and messy.

You have always loved quizzes like this, pulled from *Cosmo* or something like it, for women and girls somewhere between thirteen and thirty; they always seem so confident, so sure that there is a single right answer, and personal self-excavation is usually so very hard.

So—do you have a healthy relationship to sex?

1. When you are young, maybe five or six, you're canoeing down a river with your family—your father in the back, you in the front—and see two damselflies in the shape of a heart. You do not point them out to anyone, knowing in some way that you should be embarrassed to see this moment of intimacy. You just watch them, doing a dance that seems both wild and intimate. Do you . . .

a. Know, deep down, that they're having sex and believe that they're in love because of this?

b. Look closer and realize that the male has attached himself to her head, latched on, forcing her body to arch violently in response?

c. Realize that they are too close to the water, so close that they might drown? Do you then watch them as they submerge and never come back up?

d. All of the above.

2. You grow up watching movies about princesses and the men who love them. You dress up as them for Halloween, during playtime, whenever you can. Later it's shows like *Rock of Love* and *Flavor of Love,* reality TV where it is always women competing for men's affections. From this media intake, do you . . .

a. Learn that only beautiful women are wanted, and ugly women are jokes? Learn that if you are wanted, then that must mean you are beautiful?

b. Realize that you are the ugly duckling, not the swan? Do you ignore the ending and focus on the first part, become obsessed with your stomach, the way it rounds outwards?

c. Become overall obsessed with how you look, your crooked teeth, your stomach and thighs? Do you spend hours looking in the mirror, pinching the fat on your body until it is pricked red, like a bird whose feathers have been plucked?

d. All of the above.

3. Men lean out of their trucks and catcall you as you walk down the street, across from your high school. This has happened many times before and will happen again in other places that are meant to be safe. This intrusion, the unasked-for comments on your body, will possibly occur for the rest of your life. Do you . . .
   a. Scream "Fuck you!" at the taillights?
   b. Do nothing because it is dark and you are nervous?
   c. Secretly feel a little good about it, but then feel incredibly guilty about feeling good?
   d. All of the above.

4. At fifteen, a twenty-year-old man, a friend through a friend, tells you that you are beautiful, that if he wasn't stationed in Korea, he would teach you what it is to know a man, asks you to wait for him. Do you . . .
   a. Know in the pit of your stomach something is wrong, but let him stay because you love the attention? Do you Skype every night, strip on camera for him, let him see you in your soft youth?
   b. Spend years like this, let him call you "Jailbait" like it's something to be proud of? When he finally comes to see you, does he take you to a river to swim, and does he try to undress you there? When you say no, does he call you a tease? Do the words linger in your mind after? Do you feel like you did something wrong?
   c. Let him find you years and years later, when you are old enough to know better? Does he send you a book with a

postcard tucked inside, apologizing? Do you dream of burning it? But for some reason, do you still keep it instead, like a guilty secret you cannot find the words to name?

    d.   All of the above.

5.   Your high-school boyfriend and, at seventeen years old, your first and only real boyfriend, asks you if you want to have sex. Do you…

    a.   Say yes because you want to, because you can feel your body search for his when he's around? Do you shed any shame around the act, never look back, when you first feel his fingers push slowly inside of you while you lie across his mother's pool table?

    b.   Say yes because that's what you're supposed to do when you're in love?

    c.   Say yes because, if not now, when?

    d.   All of the above.

6.   He breaks up with you not too long after. Do you…

    a.   Know that he has always had a crush on another girl, a skinny girl, for your entire relationship and believe that the relationship is over because you are not her?

    b.   Lose your appetite because you are so heartsick and hurt?

    c.   Start to see your bones peeking out from under your skin and feel like maybe now he could really love you? In a moment of vulnerability, do you tell him that you want him in your bed again? Do you say this because it is true, or because you need to know if he would take you up on your offer?

    d.   All of the above.

7. In college, a boy puts his hand up your shirt while you watch a movie with all of your friends. Do you . . .
   a. Let him because you don't want to cause a scene?
   b. Forget it happened until years later? Let it blend into a hundred memories of men touching your body in small ways without your permission? Do the imprints of their fingers blend together, make your body realize there is a constant possibility that men may touch you without your consent and without repercussions?
   c. Spend years avoiding him without being able to explain to others why? Do you worry that you may be overreacting?
   d. All of the above.

8. For the first time in your life, you realize that men want you, really want you, and you want them. You are underage drunk, blackout drunk, and make out with strangers at parties, men with dark hair and strong hands. You feel them press hard against your hips. Do you . . .
   a. Feel powerful for your body's ability to hold men's attention? Feel good about being the kind of person men want?
   b. Feel soft and small in a way your body has never felt before? Do you imagine them holding onto your hipbone, which juts out under your skin now? Does your body tighten with excitement at the idea that you could have any of them if you wanted to?
   c. Pull back when the song is over? Do you realize people are looking at you, not him, and feel quietly ashamed for your

want? Do you wish to suddenly become like air, nowhere and everywhere all at once?

    d.   All of the above.

9.   One night, a boy who likes you and who you like too is lying in your bed, and he tries to undress you. You tell him no. He insists, continues to slide his hand up your thigh every time you push it away. *I thought you did this all the time. My friends said you were a slut,* he says. Do you . . .

    a.   Give him a lecture on the word "slut" and the anti-feminist connotations it carries?

    b.   Feel your ownership over your body slipping away? Do you realize how weak you are compared to this man, and for the first time in your life, are you genuinely afraid?

    c.   Realize for the first time the double standard at play and feel marked by it? In this moment, do you realize that you will feel stained for the rest of your time on campus, in the clothes you wear, in the organizations you join, in the makeup you choose? Do you care? Do you wish you didn't?

    d.   All of the above.

10. In college, you fall in love with a man who tells you that he loves you, but he really only loves you when you're naked. You are usually naked when you're together. He has a beautiful voice, like the sound of an upright bass. He wraps his hand around your neck during sex and leaves fingerprint bruises against your skin. When you tell him, *wait, wait, baby wait* his palm presses down. You fight all the time, break up and get back together regularly. He tells you

this is your fault—you make him crazy, *so fucking crazy*. Do you . . .

a. Tell him to fuck off, leave crying? Buy makeup to cover up any bruises, wear your hair over your neck, scarves?

b. Feel a little proud because deep down you like the idea of someone loving you so much it consumes them, makes their emotions overflow? Do you feel loved—desperately, overwhelmingly—in the way you believe you have always wanted? When you are not together, do you feel a hole in your body open up, and are you certain he's the only thing that can fill the aching emptiness?

c. Return later in the week when he promises that a fight like that, it'll never happen again?

d. All of the above.

11. It happens again. Do you . . .

a. Forgive him again?

b. And again?

c. And again?

d. And again?

12. In the breaks when you're not dating that College Man, you start going out with friends, looking for strangers to buy you drinks. You do this the summer that you're twenty, sneak into a country karaoke bar and take shots the color of rainbows. Eventually you realize you know one of the men at the bar. He was a grad student when you were a freshman; you had history class together once. Do you . . .

a. Sit next to him, let him touch your hair, smile when he says,

Wow, you look so different?

b. Sing "I Feel Lucky" by Mary Chapin Carpenter? Do you make sure to flip your hair, look at him, believe you are just so fucking good at flirting?

c. Go back to the apartment you are staying at with a friend, above a food pantry? Do you let him eat you out in the spare bedroom? Do you crawl on top of him, stretch your body out over his until your hips are aligned? Do you feel proud when after, you are both dripping with sweat, and he whispers *Wow*? For just a moment, before he gets up to leave, do you feel full?

d. All of the above.

13. Later, you go to a friend's apartment with her and a man from Tinder who buys you Crown Royal all night. You will remember nothing about the way he looks, only that he smells like liquor. Sitting between you both, he slides his hands up your thighs and hers. He stops when she starts throwing up in the bathroom, curling her body against a toilet. He takes you to the kitchen and fucks you from behind. Do you . . .

a. Throw up in the sink?

b. Joke about it later? Tell yourself that you didn't fight, didn't try to leave, if you are a victim then you are a bad one, the kind the police don't believe? Do you try your hardest to forget it ever happened?

c. Start having casual sex more often after that, always say yes to whatever they want to do to you? Does it hurt at first, and do you want it to hurt more? Do you believe that the pain will

satisfy whatever feels empty in your body, what you cannot
fill with all the drinking, all the smoking, all the drugs?

d. All of the above.

14. The man, the one from college, who held your heart between his
teeth and bit down. You get back together another time, drive three
hours to fuck him in the car outside his parents' house. He starts
to date your friend without telling you, while you're still sleeping
together. When you graduate college, you move to the city, and
he finally leaves you for the last time. He gets up and gets dressed.
He tells you, in that beautiful voice of his, that *no one will ever love
you like I do.* Do you . . .

    a. Believe him?

    b. Hate him for being the one to leave you rather than you leav-
    ing him? Do you know that it should have always been you
    doing the leaving? Do you let that resentment flower in your
    lungs until it is hard to breathe?

    c. Let him come back one more time after? Do you listen to
    him tell you how soft your lips are again, then watch him
    leave without a goodbye? Do you take a shower so hot your
    skin turns red and angry? Do you trace your lips, trying to
    understand what he felt, until they feel numb? Do you hate
    yourself for this?

    d. All of the above.

15. You start having sex with strangers again, more frequently but more
passively. You count lying down and allowing men to masturbate

with your body as "sex." You know you should use protection, but if they don't want to, you don't push it, and you don't think about it much after other than to cover the bruises that fall across your body. A friend says she's heard things, that she's worried about you. Do you . . .

a. Tell her that you think about killing yourself all the time?

b. Tell her you feel like a ghost that everyone sees? That this is the only way you know how to make your body something real?

c. Tell her that having sex is the only way to confirm you are wanted by men? Tell her that you do not want to be wanted anymore, but at the same time, desperately need to be? Do you tell her you hate that you feel this way, this jumble of emotions that don't make any sense to you?

d. None of the above. Instead, you shrug it off, tell her, *I'm fine.*

16. One morning you wake up on a mattress you have never been on before with a man you have never met before. He looks down at you from where he's standing, waking you up, with overcast eyes and a tight, thin frown of a mouth. You don't remember anything after taking a shot of tequila by the pool table at a basement bar. The soft insides of your thighs are stained a watercolor red. You are also bleeding from your rectum. Do you . . .

a. Allow him to drive you home and try not to vomit in his car? Avoid looking him in the eye, his attempts to make small talk to make it okay?

b. Vomit the moment you get home—once, twice, a third time? Do you drive an hour out to your parents' house, to be in your childhood bedroom where you feel safe?

c.   Gain weight? Do you start wearing oversized clothes? Do you dream of disappearing underwater?

d.   All of the above.

17. You try to understand what happened to you, how you seemed to fall apart into small, untethered pieces. You wake up coughing, like your body is trying to expel something from inside of you. Under free semi-professional advice, you stop having sex for a while. In this time, do you . . .

a.   Flirt relentlessly with the manager at the late-night calzone place because he always gives you free calzones but never his name? Do you appreciate that he never asks for yours?

b.   Meet a man you know is leaving town? Do you kiss him in the moonlight and say yes the first time he asks to come home with you, but do not have sex—instead curl your bodies into each other like a set of open parentheses? Do you eventually fall in love with him, in spite of the fact (or perhaps because) there are thousands of miles between you?

c.   Do you call him every night, talking about all the things you would do to each other *if only, if only*? Does he ask you to explore your body in his place, and does that make you feel good in a different way, allow you to reconnect with yourself all over again? When he comes to visit, does he make you feel like you are of your body in a way that doesn't just hurt? In this way, do you believe that you are healed?

d.   All of the above.

18. Things slowly disintegrate between you and your long-distance lover. You move across the country to a place where you know no one and spend the summer alone but not always lonely. You eventually start dating casually, slowly easing your way back into finding people who want to touch you and who you want back. You eventually begin dating just one person. You have adored before but never like this—never so fully, without fear of how it could all fall apart. Eventually, do you . . .

    a. Get into a fight while he's holding a knife? Does he throw it—not at you, per se, but does he throw it? Do you avoid him for days, tell him if it ever happens again, you're leaving? Do you mean it and feel powerful in your conviction?

    b. Do you realize that you cannot leave your past behind when it's buried in your blood, that it seeps out and leaks on everything you touch? Do you offer him a way out, tell him he can leave if he wants and you will not hold it against him? Do you feel like collapsing when he holds you instead?

    c. Ache for him to be inside you, like you have never felt for a single person before, like your bodies are magnets? Do you let him kiss down your stomach, across your stretch marks? Does his tongue speak a silent language between your thighs that leaves you desperate for him? Does he make you finally believe that maybe your body can be good?

    d. All of the above.

19. You dream of damselflies and find yourself researching them vigorously. Do you . . .

a. Learn that damselflies represent the dead? Do you worry that you're haunting yourself, that you are not meant to be this happy with someone and the ghost of yourself will ensure that this small joy you have cultivated will inevitably all come crashing down around you?

b. Learn that damselflies are surplus killers, meaning they kill and hurt not just for food but for something like fun? Do you reach for a metaphor? Do you try to philosophize about why so many men tried to kill you in so many small ways?

c. Realize that this is not about them? That they don't deserve your empathy anymore, or your willingness to justify what they did?

d. Take a long bath and cradle yourself, as naked as the day you were born? Do you offer apologies like a prayer to the belly that pushes over the water line? Do you make promises that you will not continue to punish your body for the pain it has been in? Do you hold yourself, full and alone? Do you do, as you have always done time and time again, all of the above?

In the Morning Fog

DOWN THE INTERSTATE, about twenty miles from your house, you've seen the same deer, split in half, for two days. The road is stained a deep red in long strokes, as if someone had done an aerial-view painting and decided having half of a dead deer wasn't quite dramatic enough against the grayscale days, the snow piled up on the edges of the highway, the trees still naked and bare. It is spring, technically, but a cold one.

Entrails, now rotting, fall out against the concrete. One antler is hooked onto the guard railing, its last defiant act against the cars that try to push it out of the way, the drivers that don't quite realize what they're seeing until it's too late. The rib cage is cracked open like a promise. You can't see the eyes but imagine them all black.

The morning fog offers the dead deer a cover, a casket made of clouds. This is not an unusual scene in the mountain range that makes up the twenty, fifty, hundred miles from your house. It seems half dead deer (or rather, fully dead deer, in half) are as common as the abandoned cars that litter highway edges. Sticking out of the front window are grocery bag flags, planted with the promise of return. They wave goodbye (or hello) as you drive by. You barely see either anymore.

Your hands shake when you drive—one is cold against the steering wheel and the other hot pressed to the coffee mug you bring to and from work each day. You search for some kind of physical comfort, something to hold on to against the onslaught of gray nothingness.

You work for a newspaper, and your editor is a tall man with gold-rimmed glasses and an insistence that everyone call him "Just John, thanks." He likes you because you're a good photographer and say yes to every assignment. Because you always say yes, you are often in contact with the worst parts of life—murder/suicides, fires, four-car pile-ups. You sometimes joke that now you understand why Ernest Hemingway started drinking so much when he was a journalist. You drink a lot, almost every night of the week. You said you'd stop the first time you came to work hungover, then again the first time you threw up in the employee bathroom, but you were lying both times. You keep Gatorade in the employee fridge now.

When you finally make it past the deer and into work, John sends you down the West Fork River.

The police and fire departments are there. He speaks in clipped sentences, like a telegraph come to life. *Someone saw a body last night. You need to get photographs.*

The river is thirty minutes away, and the winding road makes it feel even longer. It isn't warm enough to drive with the windows down, but you do it anyway; the air is deep and clean. You have to park in a bend on the side of the road and walk another five minutes before you see the top of the fire truck, burning red, a flaming match against a smoky sky.

There is no missing person's report that fits the description. *It was likely a homeless man,* the fire chief speculates. His firefighters had seen the body in the water.

I believe my men, he says.

It goes like this for a week: every day, to and from work, you pass the deer. Every few days, you're sent back to take more photos. There is still no body. The chief invites you to peer into the water, but all you can see is your own reflection, turned dark and blurry.

You used to feed deer from the palm of your hand, allowed them to lick the salt of your skin. Once, when you were young enough to still be brave, you stroked the fuzz of a new antler on a fawn. Sometimes you still dream of him, the way he looked at you, with the big brown eyes, the color of the earth itself. You had not realized that deer had eyelashes. When he blinked, you were startled.

In the dream, he eats from your hand again, and his tongue is warm. It is not technically a nightmare—you know this logically—but when you wake in the middle of the night, you are covered in sweat and panting, the air around you stale.

A week becomes a month and still, no body. The fog eventually lifts, but the air carries the taste of winter. You half dream about dying all the time, about drowning, about running away. The deer fades into the background of your memory. Life goes on in a stilted, slow way.

It isn't until the end of May that they find a body, only able to be called that by the loosest of terms. By then it's been soaked into nothingness by its temporary tomb.

The autopsy is inconclusive, the chief tells you when you call to write up your final report. *Nothing but bones.*

By then there is another dead deer on your way to and from work. You barely take stock of its death until John sends you out to cover a crime scene, a crooked standing house where a man pushed a woman down the stairs and broke her back in half, painted her purple and blue.

You drive slowly past the deer and note the darkness its skin has become, how it was ripped open by birds and made a home to maggots.

You think of the half bottle of vodka waiting for you in your freezer, the color of ice.

After you pass by, you turn to look at your hands against the steering wheel; it's then you realize they've been stained by the newspaper ink turning your fingers ashen and gray. You grip the wheel tighter and drive on.

INCANTATIONS OF LEAVING

THERE ARE no eyes of newt dropped into bubbling cauldrons while chanting, no real magic to the affair. Sometimes you wish there was something more ritual about the leaving of lovers. That might be easier, or at least more palpable in the aftermath, if there was a clear-cut moment between The Before and The End.

You reach for the power of trying to make your harm yours, not just something people do to you. You learn these incantations, things people have said to you, and try to make them fit your mouth. After all, no matter how much being left hurts, it is incomparable to the tidal wave that comes with being alone.

You take their being gone personally. You write their words on paper to rip them up and throw them away. You feel like a spiral of water running down a drain. You create bad poetry about your open arms—how they outstretch into endlessness—and your open mouth—how you are not able to do anything more than parrot back others' words, how silly you believe you are for always being the one left behind.

I'm not looking for anything serious in a relationship.
You come to believe that seriousness is something that no one is actually looking for at all but rather an event that simply happens to someone, like falling. You begin to believe that you can transform yourself into

the kind of seriousness that they want. You will be wrong, of course. You will tell yourself that you are not looking for anything serious either. That you do not need an anchor, and that you are not desperately reaching for anything that looks like the ground. Repeat these things until they sound like truth.

I'm still in love with (fill in blank).

Your lover's chest sounds like seashell. You do not hate them or their hermit crab heart, but you do envy the person who was able to leave a mark on someone that feels so impermanent. Happiness feels like trying to trap sand between your fingers.

When he forgets to come to the dinner you prepared for him, pour the $10 wine down the sink. Leave the food out as a sacrificial offering to the heartache that still haunts him.

I'm leaving soon.

You constantly feel like you are up to your lungs in water and your lifejacket was left on the shore.

To help with the pain, put a ring of salt around your bed (or a series of pretzels you get from the Walgreens around the corner, where you buy them in bulk) and lie down.

Do not leave it for two days, even if your roommates start to worry you may be "having an episode."

It's not the right time.

Like a chant repeated so often that the words break down into nothing more than syllables. Time breaks down and becomes blurry, as if you are wearing glasses that aren't yours.

When you get so drunk that your memories must be recounted back to you like a story, know that this is what it means to live outside of your body, outside of time. In an attempt to escape out of the wrong time and into the right one, do it again and again and again.

You deserve better than me.
Dream of waves pushing forward and back, always loving and leaving. Visit the ocean, a river, a lake, or even an exceptionally large puddle. Drop pebbles in the water to forget about how badly you want to pretend to fall in and drown to feel connected to someone, something, anything other than the endless cavern of loneliness in your ribcage.

[silence, followed by a deep breath]
.

.

.

Make hot milk with ashwagandha to induce sleep.
Tuck a fluorite stone into bed with you to make your room feel deep—oceanic, even, your mattress a raft.
Gargle saltwater to help heal the cuts on the inside of your lower lip, where your bones have grinded against your own soft, pink insides.
These are tips you found on Google and barely believe in, but the hopelessness brings with it a kind of faith you do not agree with in any other state of being.

I just don't love you.
Sleep.

Dream of becoming a ghost that haunts a seashore that is thousands of miles away.

Call in sick to work.

When you finally go outside it will be the middle of the day, when everyone else in the neighborhood is gone. It will feel as quiet and unknown as the witching hour. The sunlight coming in through the leaves in your backyard will decorate your face and turn your cheeks warm. Somewhere, you hear children laughing. This will be the day you realize that you can't live here anymore, in the bounds of a city where every corner carries a memory of a pain you don't yet know how to vocalize.

Someday, you will realize that you didn't love any of these men— you just wanted them to love you enough for both of you.

PART TWO: THE REGENERATION

Forgotten Synonyms for Grief

"We admit that we are like apes, but we seldom realize that we are apes."

—*Richard Dawkins*

WANT (verb). From Old Norse, *vanta,* "to lack."

Meaning: to not have.

Meaning: if there is a want, it must mean there is a lack.

Meaning: Wanting someone who will never exist again means there is a hole in the fabric of the space.

Meaning: I learn I must live with the emptiness in my chest the way the universe learns to live with black holes.

Example: I want a dog for years before I actually get one. The lack of an animal in my house becomes more pressing when I run away from my hometown for grad school. At least, it feels like running away, perhaps because I had never lived more than forty-five minutes from my parents before. I leave because I realize that I want more than a life that feels like it is slipping through my fingers, spending all my time thinking of dying and drinking in basement bars. Home is too small, and I want to burst out of it, to do something dramatic and big. But change is hard, even if you know it's supposed to be good in the long run.

It is the first time I live in a place where I am not related to at least three other residents, and I am deeply lonely in my one-bedroom apartment with its high ceilings and tall windows that make me feel naked and vulnerable. I spend most of my time alone, talking into the air.

It feels empty in a way I cannot fill with art or furniture, and I spend the nights I am not in class avoiding going home. I think of a man I once called a brother, dead for years now. I see Dillon often, a mirage on every motorcycle, and have nightmares of the day he crashed. I listen to bluegrass music, songs that remind me of home, often listening to an old recording of Dillon trying to play "Ole Slew Foot," always two beats too slow. I write frantic letters to him but burn them on the front porch before I ever finish one. I feel like I am searching for something, without knowing what it is.

A few weeks after what would have been Dillon's birthday, I decide on a whim to finally get a dog. I go to the shelter hoping for a senior pet that I can make comfortable for a few years. Instead, I leave with a puppy who shakes in the concrete kennel. The shelter volunteers tell me she has recently been split up from her sister, and I am drawn to her in ways I can't explain.

After I take her into my home, she is sick for days. *Kennel cough,* the vet tells me when I rush her in, terrified I have done something fatally wrong. *Nothing serious.*

I do not believe her. My dog avoids me at first, hides under my couch as I try to coax her out with food. When she does eat, she throws up. She is already small, no more than twelve pounds, and I worry she will continue to shrink until she disappears. I am convinced she is not sick from kennel cough but rather from the brokenhearted ache that comes from being left behind, and I become irrationally terrified she will die on my watch. I get scared to leave my house longer than a trip to the grocery store.

The first night she joins me in my bed, I lay awake with my hands cupped around her ribs. Her fur is fine and soft, and through her skin I can outline the delicate bones that hold her together. Her breathing is shallow, and I realize how much I love her, this small creature who knows nothing of me except that I am all she has now. It is terrifying—to love something so much and be aware that it could all shatter.

Example: In 1983, Koko the gorilla asked for a kitten for Christmas. When she was given a stuffed animal instead, she was aware that it was not real. She would not play with it and continued to sign "SAD" over and over again until her birthday in July. It was then that she was able to pick from a litter of abandoned kittens, take one for her own. She chose a gray male Manx, named him "All Ball" and nurtured him as if he was a baby gorilla. That is, with tenderness. That is, she cared for him.

Later that year, All Ball escaped and was hit by a car. When Koko was told that her cat was dead, she signed "BAD, SAD, BAD" and "FROWN, CRY, FROWN, SAD, TROUBLE." Her custodian later noted that he could hear her making sounds similar to human weeping. Gorillas cannot cry. But she wanted to.

Testify (verb). From Late Middle English, *testis,* "a witness."

Meaning: give evidence as a witness.

Meaning: To be there.

Meaning: To be able to share.

Example: Koko taught Michael, another gorilla, several signs. They became best friends, painting together, listening to music, telling stories. They both used the signs "stink" for "flowers" and "lip" for "girl."

Michael's mother was killed by poachers. When he was asked what he remembered about her, he told them this of her death: "SQUASH MEAT GORILLA. MOUTH TOOTH. CRY SHARP-NOISE LOUD. BAD THINK-TROUBLE LOOK-FACE. CUT/NECK LIP (GIRL) HOLE."

Example: Dillon died in a motorcycle accident. The embalming fluid would have flushed out the yellow undertones of his skin, turned him too white. I had seen it in corpses before. He flipped the motorcycle and met the cement face first. Or maybe there wouldn't have been a body there at all. Perhaps instead there was an urn with him and his teeth and his hair all reduced to ash and earth. I don't know. I didn't go to Dillon's funeral, so I never found out.

Lack (noun). From Middle Dutch *laken,* or "lack, blame."

Meaning: the state of being without.

Meaning: If you were to yell into a black hole, would anyone hear it?

Meaning: Holes occupy an unusual position in human psychology. We tend to refer to them as tangible and countable objects, something that exists, when in fact holes are an absence of something else.

Example: I have attended many funerals in my life, most of them for people younger than me and nearly all of them men. Funerals give me an itch in a way I know they are not supposed to. I prefer to keep my griefs quiet and internal; comfort makes me uncomfortable. When I stand next to fellow mourners, the heat of my palms pressed to a stranger's as we clasp our hands together in silence, I know I should feel something communal. But I only ever find my own lonely heartbeat in my throat.

Funerals themselves do not make me sad—I feel that deep, terrible grief at random times, like in the middle of the grocery store years later, when I see a man with Dillon's hair, dark and curly, and forget how to breathe in the dog food aisle.

Funerals make me lonely. They remind me of the original desire carved into my psyche, to always want another breath, then another, then another. It seems like I am in a constant state of desire; I am a stretched arm, an open palm, a hungry mouth. I have tried to fill the hole in my chest with new clothes, with food, with wine, with sex, with liquor, with work, with drugs. I have tried to make myself satisfied by these things. I feel that longing to be full more acutely at funerals than I do anywhere else.

The day Dillon's funeral happened, I drove up to the closest thing we had for a city and went to a series of dive bars with strangers, trying to drink enough to make me forget what I was missing. I danced and laughed at bad jokes. I smoked an entire pack of cigarettes, one after the other, tasting the nicotine on my tongue before I swallowed it. I wanted to feel alive—shimmeringly, painfully alive. It felt selfish because it was. When we grieve, is it for them? Or for us, who now have to live without them? It didn't matter then. I had never felt so absolutely alone before, convinced that I could disappear in the night and no one would notice.

Example: Dorothy was thirty when she died at the Sanaga-Yong Chimpanzee Rescue Centre in eastern Cameroon. Workers knew she was an important figure to the other resident chimpanzees but weren't sure how they would perceive her death—or if they would at all. The twenty-five other chimps were famously loud and boisterous, as easily excitable as children.

When workers went to get Dorothy, they wrapped her corpse in a blanket and placed her in a wheelbarrow. As they rolled by, all the other chimps stood at the edge of the perimeter and watched in complete silence, their hands on their brethren's shoulders. They comforted one another. They reminded each other that they were still alive. They made note of the absent space she left behind.

Need (verb). Coming from Middle English *nede*, originally it is "violence, force."

Meaning: what is required, wanted, or desired.

Meaning: to be so desperate for something, it feels like a violence.

Example: Washoe the chimp had a caretaker named Kat, who was pregnant one day and then not the next. She took time off, and when she returned to Washoe, the chimp was upset that she had been abandoned. Kat decided to tell Washoe the truth, signing, "MY BABY DIED."

Washoe had lost two infants herself—the first to a heart defect shortly after birth; the second, a staph infection when she was two months old. The second baby was named Sequoyah.

What did Washoe feel then?

What does it mean to share your grief?

Example: After I see the ghost of Dillon in the supermarket, I leave all my groceries in the cart in the middle of the aisle. I slip out to my car and curl my body forward, my head on my knees. I don't know how long I live like this—maybe a few minutes, maybe an hour. Time becomes isolated and still. I do not cry; I relearn how to breathe in silence. In. Out. In. Out. In. Out.

How do we survive grief so terrible it feels like a razor in your stomach, like looking over the edge of the universe? We do it for the others who need us. I drive home and greet my dog at the door. I turn the radio on and Johnny and June Cash sing "Ole Slew Foot" to me, and I laugh so hard I start crying and my dog starts barking, and then it is just one noise, both of us trying to say something without words or language but in how intensely we feel everything.

Example: Washoe turned to Kat. She brought her finger up to her eye and dragged it down her cheek, signing "CRY," signaling where the tears should have been. I imagine it was quiet as they focused on their breathing. I want to believe there was a comfort between them as it became one universal animal sound.

Becoming Fireflies

I WANT YOU to make me a promise—after we say our final goodbyes, after I drive away from your house in the middle of the night for the last time, after our time together has begun to go dark around the edges of your memory—after all this, you will start committing petty crimes. If you will bike in the wrong lane and flip off the cars that honk at you, I will jaywalk at every possible opportunity. If you steal Chapstick every time you go to a Walmart or Winn-Dixie or any other chain store life might take you, I will do the same.

I have come to terms with the fact that forever isn't meant for us, not in this lifetime. Some relationships are just like that. When we first met, you told me you were leaving soon, and despite that I still thought you could offer some kind of salvation to the life I was passing through. I was living under the romantic notion that the miles didn't matter, that love would conquer all our differences. It is no one's fault. We are a set of perpendicular lines, meant to meet and then continue on the different paths we are both determined to take.

This is something you have known for a while now, and it took me awhile but I understand now. It has been two years since we first met, and through it all—the late-night phone calls, the weekend visits, you moved, I moved, farther and farther apart each time—time seems to have bent around our forms. It never could have lasted. Time isn't meant to be elastic like that, not for too long—eventually, it must snap back into place.

But I have a theory that I can only test with you. I hope that maybe, if we become small-time criminals for the next fifty years, reincarnation will see fit that we return to this world as bugs. And if we're really lucky, if we commit just the right number of tiny injustices, we will become fireflies at the same time.

Imagine it.

It is winter now, and perhaps because of these never-ending gray days, I have started to romanticize the future of our summer together. I'll be born wild, by the river where we first met. If I come back into this world at dusk, I may have the good fortune to be caught in the soft hands of a child who has only just come to understand what it means to hold an entire lifetime in her palms only to be released and find you again. Do this with me, and I will find you.

What are two weeks to a firefly? A lifetime together.

And what can be held in any lifetime?

When we are nothing more than insects, I can only hope that time will no longer have meaning or weight. There will be no fear of the future because there will be no future. No waiting. No maybes. No somedays. I believe if we do this, our bodies will be able to hold on to the muscle memory of how we slept together when the snow kept us inside, naked and vulnerable. In this way, we can bend time to our needs, live in the small moments that felt like they could stretch into our own personal eternity.

In A Parallel Universe, Perhaps We Never Meet and Are Worse Off Because of It

1.

We met at a bar on a Thursday, where shots were 50 cents. I was out with co-workers, other women in their early twenties, and we had made friends with men who kept following us, bar to bar, and would not leave no matter how we tried to shake them. The man was taller than me, and I had tried to tell him to leave, and he hadn't taken the suggestion well or with any seriousness. I was hoping to quite literally ghost him somewhere between the bathroom, the dance floor, and the bar.

So I was hiding from someone else when I slid up to the bar and met you. You were thin and wore glasses, and I knew I had matched with you on Tinder several months prior but had never spoken to you before. You seemed safe.

Hi, I need you to pretend that we have been involved in a deep conversation. I'm avoiding someone, I told you. Do you remember this? Later I would understand how much you loved the ridiculousness of this, how you were always up for some kind of adventure.

Then, you just said, *Okay. Do you want a shot?*

I did. So all night, we took shots, and we ended up sleeping together in my friend's attic, where you rubbed my feet and together we fell asleep under one blanket.

2.

Maybe a lot of things could have been avoided if I had put my foot down earlier, told you that I wasn't going to pretend to be your girlfriend if I wasn't.

Except we loved pretending we were together even if we weren't. You moved away just two weeks after we first met. We didn't use words like *commitment* or *together* or *love*. We disagreed often about the future. I didn't believe in the military. You had dreamed of being a pilot since you first heard the words. But we drank more than we disagreed. And I loved getting drunk and holding hands under the bar, loved spending long weekends going out to restaurants we couldn't afford, loved making out at 2 a.m. on those winter nights where anyone could have seen us between the snow flurries that stuck to your shoulders and melted in my hair.

I loved the safety of the weekends you came to visit me in West Virginia, how they felt like small worlds contained inside a larger universe. I could pretend to be someone I wasn't then. We didn't talk about how I was always sleeping with strangers, how much I wanted to die every winter, how I imagined burying myself under the snow to forget all the strangers' hands that had made what was supposed to be mine theirs.

With you, I could pretend I was happy all the time. I could pretend to be laid-back and fun and in love. You allowed me my fantasies. Each visit was an individual snow globe of time on the shelf of my memory. It can be shaken and moved, but not changed.

3.

When you were at basic, I saw you just that one time in person. I flew in for a wedding a few towns over. You came down to share a hotel room. You told me of the windowless rooms, how much you missed the outside world. The hotel looked out at the Rocky Mountains. You told me you missed the hills we had met in. I wanted to tell you that I missed you more than the hills, but I didn't. That felt like the kind of seriousness that we had silently agreed not to engage in. But that night I held you, warm skin to warm skin.

4.

Once I left West Virginia, you never came to visit me again. But after basic training, I went to spend a weekend at your temporary Texas address. I was still pretending that maybe we would one day sort it all out, that we could still have a fulfilling relationship, two golden retrievers, a house, friends we didn't hate—drinking problems left behind and forgotten.

The second night, we got drunk and you took me to the Alamo. It was summer, and the air had a flat kind of heat. I met your military friends and your intramural rugby team, and I smiled and laughed at the right jokes, relaxed into your arms when they wrapped around my waist.

I still have a copy of that picture of us in front of the Alamo. It's all lit up in the back. You're in a long-sleeved flannel, your hand stretched over my body, and you're looking down at me. My head is tilted up at yours. We are both laughing. We look so truly happy in this moment that now, years later, it still makes me smile.

When we were done drinking, we took an Uber to get tacos from a gas station. It was you, me, and two of your friends. I don't remember how you knew them.

You sat in the front.

Your friend stuck his hand down my shirt in the back seat.

It is the only completely clear memory I have of that trip.

All the other pieces are hazy movements. The taste of a cocktail, the smell of your shampoo, the sound of laughter. But your friend's hand is branded into the memory. The car had stopped suddenly and pushed our bodies forward, and your friend forced his hand into my shirt, his cold hand against my breast, and he squeezed—and I didn't say anything I was so surprised.

I was supposed to be safe with you.

When I told you after, you didn't say that you thought I was lying, but you did say *I can't believe he would do that.*

I really believed it, that I was going to be safe with you.

My illusions of the *us* that had never existed were shattered. How could I live life like this? We had been Not Together for years by then. That night it felt like I was stepping out into the morning after having been awake all night and saw the fireflies for what they really are: just a bunch of bugs. Everything is so much harsher in the light, isn't it?

5.

In another universe, we could have ended in a big explosion that was filled with screaming and broken plates and busted bloody egos, like the one we saw in that other movie whose name I forget because I was drunk when we watched it on that final day in Texas, when the air between us was suddenly stiff and harsh.

This is to say: maybe we could have split up in a way that felt final like that instead of drifting apart in the way people do, like two floating rings carried in different directions by the ocean, each able to see the other but never touch again.

Maybe in that other universe we wouldn't check in on each other still then, call and talk on the phone here and there to remind ourselves of when we were young and stupid and so in love that it swelled up big in our bodies and we had no idea what to do with it.

I need you to know that I'm okay. In fact, I am okay in part because of you, not despite. I was so happy in those snow globe moments that I think eventually by pretending so much, it just started happening for real.

I still smile at that photo of us at the Alamo, don't I? Those people are like strangers now, but I think of them fondly—of how flawed they were, of how much they wanted others to save them when really, they were just learning how to trust others to fail and be okay anyways.

6.

Sometimes I wonder if you still talk to that friend. Do you ever talk about me? Don't tell me if you do. If the answer is yes, I would prefer not to know. I no longer care if you forgave him on my behalf, without my permission, by virtue of never making him face the consequences of his entry to my body.

This is a promise I have seen so many men make, a fraternity of quietness—sure, you may agree, *that was messed up*. But he's still your friend. Don't worry. I have forgiven you for this. Or maybe *forgiven* isn't the right word: I don't care anymore. The light friendship we carry doesn't go that deep now. We don't talk about things like that. We just talk about how hot it is lately and how much we've changed.

In this universe, you do things like recommend a beer you're sure I'll just love, and I know that when I try it I will like it, but something will be slightly off—it will taste like something I would have enjoyed years ago, when I had worse taste.

Bar Bathroom Graffiti in New Orleans: A One-Year Catalog

"Don't Worry Dear, I Forgive You!"—Jan. 1, R Bar

It feels good to go into a new year knowing that someone, somewhere, has forgiven me for all that I am and all I've done. In this moment the bathroom nearly feels like a confessional, as if I can speak to the walls in this single stall and reveal the worst parts of myself. As long as I come back, I will be forgiven again and again, no conditions attached.

This is actually often how I feel in bar bathrooms, a step away from people and noise and all that encompasses. I like to observe graffiti, see the stalls become galleries, find out what people are yelling into the universe. Sometimes I like to think it's just for me. I've never written anything myself, but I understand the urge to create something that feels permanently heard.

"Impeach Kavanaugh"—Jan. 2, Banks St. Bar

It's only been a few months since the Kavanaugh hearings, and the very private wound, felt collectively, is still dangerously open.

The summer I was fourteen I tripped on gravel, and the skin of my knees opened up to show the world my insides. When it happened, first I screamed at the blood on the rocks, then I laughed, and then I was doing both; I couldn't help myself. The camp nurse comforted me and applied Neosporin and wrapped my body back inside itself.

Weeks after I peeled off the Ace bandage, I still picked at the bubbles of individual scabs left behind, let them open over and over again until my mother started to question how they hadn't healed yet and whether she should take me to a medical professional. My father assured her it was my fault; I was the one keeping them red and alive. Only then did I let them scar.

This time it's not me picking at the scab, but I carry the guilt of it all the same, the invisible open gash of living in a woman's body that other people have tried to claim as their own. It feels good to see that even in bar bathrooms, someone is offering what feels like a tender touch across the walls.

The entirety of "When Death Comes" and an excerpt of "Wild Geese" by Mary Oliver—Jan. 18, 12 Mile

We're out drinking because the poet Mary Oliver was alive two days ago and dead the day after, and the world seemed worse all at once. There are already two tributes to the poet from two different people, separate handwriting on the same wall honoring one woman. For a moment, it feels like we are all holding hands, collectively grieving—if not for her, for someone else, even if it was just ourselves.

Throughout the year, I will continue to return to the shrine. "You do not have to be good," her writing urges me, reminds me, tries to tell me something I don't quite understand the importance of yet. "You only have to let the soft animal of your body love what it loves."

I read over the last line of "When Death Comes," and I touch it after I wash my hands: "I don't want to end up simply having visited this world."

What does the soft animal of my body love? What does any animal want? I wonder what it is to visit the world, what it is to live, and if I'll ever be able to figure out the difference. It feels like we're all just dominos trying to topple into each other to create something meaningful, some way to be heard. I worry nothing I've created is good enough to last. But does it matter?

"It Is In Your Self-Interest To Find A Way To Be Very Tender"—Feb. 20, ???

The first "e" in "Tender" is scratched out, so it almost looks like "Tinder" instead, which I like nearly as much. I am very drunk when I first read this, which is why I don't know where it is, but I continue to look for it many times.

"BANSHEE BANSHEE BANSHEE"—Feb. 21, Santos

The text, all caps, screams against the wall.

The music, heavy and full of guitars, screams back.

I want to scream too.

Banshee feels like a loaded word for a woman and because of that, I like it. It's probably a band name or something, but that doesn't matter. The walls are thin, and the bass of the music penetrates into the back room, where women talk about men and offer strangers their lipstick. Outside the bathroom door, through the dance floor and over to the bar, a man I think I could spend a lot of time with buys me a drink. Alex and I have been on just enough dates that I've lost count but not so many that the newness of dating has worn off. He's lived in the city long enough that he can take me to bars I haven't been to yet, and I am new enough to New Orleans that I am still impressed by this.

I still feel like I have to impress him. I like to revel in that caring, the excitement of learning someone new. It presses against my chest when he looks at me, the want that comes with it; I worry he won't want me when I become human, when he learns and understands who I am, when everything stops being casual and fun. I know it has to happen eventually, but I just want him to stay long enough to find out.

I make my way over to the bar and take the drink he has picked out for me. Alex comes from a beachside town, and his hair looks like an ocean's breaking point. He is a music journalist, and most of our dates are to see bands I've never heard of at bars where everyone seems cooler than me. No matter where we go, he seems to know someone. He is always well dressed in westerns and button-downs, classic cuts that make it clear he cares about what he wears and how he wears it. He walks with one foot pointed inwards, and his eyes are the color of spring grass. He looks at me in a way that makes me believe he is truly listening. I like being with him in a simple, easy way, and that's terrifying.

DO YOU WANT TO GO BACK TO MY PLACE, he has to yell over the music.

YES, I say, and take his hand, letting him pull me from out of my own head and onto the street outside.

"We Eat Gumbo Because It's Great"
—Feb. 23, Circle Bar

It's in the thick of carnival season, and I am always having fun and always tired, waking up with glitter in my bed even though it hasn't been on my body in weeks, and I swear I keep washing the sheets. In my dreams, there's music, and I eat so much that it feels decadent. I feel like I could be in love, just a little bit—with the man, with the city, with the constant feeling that the community is on the precipice of something wonderful. Beads hang from the trees by my house like the Spanish moss. Time blurs in a way that makes me feel like I am holding a glass figurine in my hands— that there is something so deeply precious in my grasp, and if I am too intent and squeeze it or if I am too relaxed and drop it, it could all shatter.

"God and I have become like two giant fat people living in a tiny boat. We keep bumping into each other and laughing —Hafiz"
—Feb. 28, somewhere on Frenchmen

I haven't prayed in a long time, but I like the idea of finding a god on accident, in places that don't just feel serious and devout—I want to touch something holy in places that make me laugh too. My grandfather is a pastor, but at this point I've been avoiding church longer than I ever attended.

The writing is in chalk. Someone will erase it by morning—I'm sure of it. Taking a picture feels like my way of telling god that I'm listening, I'm preserving.

"Sister Act 2: Back In the Habit Is Far Superior to the Original Film"—July 6, Gasa Gasa

It's written across the entire door, this all-important message. In the corner, someone has added "The Shrek trilogy too!" I start laughing and so does the other woman in the bathroom, and we each take a picture of it.

A few weeks later, I find out my uncle is dead. He's told he's dying on Wednesday and does it on Sunday. That night I sob without breathing on my boyfriend's bed. He offers to drive me into the depths of the swamps so we can look at stars. It takes us an hour to get there, and we sit on the edge of the bank, the sky open and empty.

It's going to be okay, Alex says.
I know, I say. *It's just not right now. I'm not okay.*

On the drive back, I try to find a picture on my phone to show him and see this graffiti instead, the text loud and excited. I start to laugh and it becomes crying, and I somehow do both at the same time.

I eventually return to the bathroom shrine to Mary Oliver. What animal have I become? I take my dog to the park, and we watch the geese there. At night I dream of them, large and loud, always in pairs. The heat makes the days blend. Life feels stagnant, and that makes me worry that

I am too. I consider throwing away all my clothes, selling my couches, quitting everything that ties me to one single place and driving as far as I can, until I feel like I am inside myself again.

"~~impeach~~ Assassinate Kavanaugh"
—Aug. 7, Banks St. Bar

I like the change. My personal wound feels like it's begun to scar over, and I want to pick at it again and again. I have become comfortable, less angry, and that can feel like complicity. It's so exhausting, holding onto that violence. But I don't want to heal. I don't want to forget.

I tell Alex bits and pieces of my personal history. I explain the nightmares about men whose names I never learned. I have a panic attack when I go for a walk alone and have to cross the path of four men on the street. He holds me after. It still feels like my fault.

"Don't let a sad boi / boy / girl / woman / person get you down. It ain't fucking worth it, 'sides the self-inspection"—Sept. 13, The Other Bar

We are going to a show at Gasa Gasa, but we stop by The Other Bar first, and I don't know if these omnipotent instructions are for me or someone else. I try to follow the writing's commandment and consider if other people get me down, and decide that really, it seems like maybe I'm the one making myself sad.

Despite the moving seasons, the leaves barely change, and the temperature still holds the summer's heat.

"Magic is real + it lives in your ~~hearts~~ CUNTS"
—Sept.13, Gasa Gasa

This one makes me laugh, and I feel grounded again.

"Move to New Orleans, Forget Your Old Life, Talk to Ghosts"—Nov. 8, Circle Bar

I've lived in New Orleans long enough to impress people with my bar recommendations. I buy a book of Mary Oliver's poetry and immediately lose it. I haven't prayed in a long time, but tonight I find the soft animal of my body and god in the bathroom together, and I laugh and dance with a man who loves me when I'm so human it hurts. I tell the ghosts in my life how much I love them. I forgive myself.

THE COLLAPSING OF
HUMMINGBIRDS' NESTS

RIGHT AFTER we met, I bought a piece of painted glass—an oval framed in metal with two hummingbirds and flowers painted on it. It depicts the birds close to life-size, each with a wingspan smaller than the length of my finger, their bodies a pair of parentheses hovering in mid-air. One is looking up at the chandelier of pink and white flowers that hangs above their small bodies. If you look closely, the second hummingbird seems to be looking at its partner. How could the gaze be described? Like love? Maybe concern? It depends on what day I look at it.

I once read that there is meaning behind the first thing you bring into a new home, that it sets an intention. Certainly, this painted piece of glass was not the first thing I brought over to purposely leave behind; that was probably a toothbrush—a purple, plastic flag in your bathroom that proclaimed the seriousness of our relationship during its uncertain beginnings. I fell in love with New Orleans while I fell in love with you, and the hummingbirds were the first thing I brought over after we decided your house would be ours, here in the center, beating heart of the city.

Hummingbirds don't have traditional homes, the strong twig-based nests you might think of birds using. Instead, they create small cups from leaves and plant fibers, using spider silk to hold them together. Their nests are meant to be able to stretch as the residents grow, and once they grow enough, the home collapses. Of course, not every species is as careful as the next; some hummingbirds make their nests loose, almost to the point of precariousness, tying their homes to clotheslines. Imagine it: waking up one day, taking your laundry outside, and finding a hummingbird nest where your shirt should be.

Because they lack the load-bearing columns of hard twigs, the nests are incredibly fragile; they will bend and break, fall apart when faced with almost any kind of turmoil. For nests to last longer than a single season is something close to a miracle.

The idea that we'll ever grow out of this one-bedroom apartment where the kitchen sink doesn't work right, where there is a hole in the bathroom that's only covered by a painting you put up, where all of our books have joined one collection—the idea of leaving is unimaginable. I didn't like the apartment very much at first; it seemed that it always had some problem or another.

But now I walk through our home, looking at the tomato plants you've grown in the corner, their flowers small and yellow, unpollinated still; the flyers for concerts we attended that you stole from coffee shops, framed and hung up next to the painting my sister made when we moved in together; the Polaroid stuck to the fridge that shows you drunk and smiling, laughing at a joke I said then but no longer remember. I realize I've grown into this space, and now I worry that we will continue to grow until it breaks around us.

Sometimes we joke that we'll sell everything and live out of a van one day, traveling together. Or that we'll buy a big house on the beach and spend every day by the ocean. The road in front of us is open and wide with so many directions that I get dizzy trying to look at them all. In this way I imagine our life beyond these walls like a daydream; an actual future with you feels ungraspable right now.

It's not because I don't want it. To be honest, I always thought we would break in half—into pieces of sharp, shattered glass—before we made it this far. We have both been in past relationships that have fallen apart. After I moved in with you, I was always on edge, fearing that the next thunderstorm would be our destruction. And yes, living in a city below sea level means every rain brings fears of flooding, but I love sitting together on the balcony, watching the street become an ocean.

Now that I have settled into this home, I am afraid of what the next move might bring, that we could leave this place and fall apart without it. In this way it seems like we only survive in the present, within the everyday moments that pass between us like secrets. It is in coffee waiting at my desk in the morning, in the open-palmed touch when your hand finds my body in the middle of the night, in the way we live in an apartment with windows that make every time of day feel like sunrise.

How can this be sustainable outside of the small world that we have created?

How will we ever leave a place where my hummingbirds can hang on a balcony hook?

Every year, a ruby-throated hummingbird, like the kind we have suspended in glass, will migrate back to the same spot. They fall in love with a place, and though they may leave it, they will return to their homes time and time again. The migration process is a particularly vicious one; in the spring they fly nonstop across the Gulf of Mexico. In good weather, they can go for six hundred miles at a time. The process kills many of them, but it makes those that survive it even stronger.

All of this is to say: As much as I want to hide in these moments, these small daily miracles, I know that time and death are the only inevitables in life. I want you to know that though I am scared, I will go anywhere with you.

Tell me that you will not outgrow me, and I will promise you that should we fall apart, it will not be our destruction; that we can create homes together for the rest of our lives. We can sell everything and travel across the country, hang our hummingbirds up in the back seat of a van and listen to the glass rattling against the window as we drive. We can buy a big house by the beach and spend our days trying to cross the Gulf of Mexico. We can build a treehouse together. Construct it so precariously: set upon the branches, it will be as if it were built from spider webs on laundry lines. And when one inevitably falls apart, we can build another one, and then another, and then another.

First, There Was the Comb Jelly

I N THE BEGINNING, there was only darkness. Then the waters. Then there was light. Genesis 1:1 and my grandfather tell me that the condition of the world when god took hold of it was untamed and shapeless, until he said, "Let there be light." This, of course, implies that there was a world prior to god, a world of darkness and wild waters, long before those with power started claiming the great everything—first the mountains, the rivers, then later the oceans, and eventually the cosmos themselves.

But I cannot help but think of those days before—when it was only night and only water. What roamed the earth then?

I think of the comb jelly.

Until pretty recently, scientists believed that the first animal, in the traditional way we think of animals, was a sea sponge. A basic, simple creature capable only of survival. It would make sense, wouldn't it? That the tree of life, the hierarchy of evolutionary movements and relationships, would begin with the basics.

At the start, there was only darkness. And the sea sponge.

However, a recent turn of events has us reconsidering who the first, the original, animal may have been. New research from scientists at Brown University has determined that it could be the shockingly complex comb jelly sitting at the base of the tree of life. It is a new origin story for all of the world.

In one of my first memories, my parents took my sisters and me to the beach, somewhere along the Atlantic. We ran in and out of the ocean, screaming and laughing as we plunged our bodies into the water before running back out again. It was a game we played, chasing the movement of the tides, following the white surf of the water as it disappeared against the shore over and over again. Sometimes I ran out deeper than I could stand and dove underwater and shut my eyes, allowed my body to be rocked and moved by the water until at last I popped up and swam back to shore again. At the time, my body felt weightless and alive.

My mother read on the beach, though she stopped to check on us now and then to make sure that we had not found a way to sink under the ocean. I know my father was there, but in my memory, I don't know where. He moved like the surf, vanishing past the edge of existence yet still vital to the memory.

This was my genesis story—my mother and father, who gave me darkness, then light, then water to swim and play and live in. Over time I learned this came with a weight too. Like all parents, my mother and father had expectations for their children, societal expectations and desires for us to grow into competent young people who would be able to forge a life of our own one day. There was never time for resting; we were always striving for something.

I took music lessons. Played sports. Tutored. Worked in the summer. Joined extracurriculars. Volunteered at the local food pantry, then the library. Went to a good college. Continued volunteering. Joined more organizations. Took leadership positions. Added more scholarships, more majors, more and more and more. I felt the weight of my parents' expectations around my neck like an invisible anchor. I began to develop a hunch, my back and shoulders tired.

You should never be satisfied, my father told me once. *You can always be better.*

I imagine floating in the ocean alone, hiding in the darkness of the water, my body moved only by the push and pull of the ocean, shapeless and untamed.

The comb jelly is not a true jellyfish like how some may think of them now—floating, bell-shaped creatures with long, stinging tentacles, perfectly safe until they're not. Looking at images of the comb jelly, however, you can see early traces of what the jellyfish would become. They have the same soft body and small tentacles. The would-be limbs look like baby teeth, not quite in their full form, but hold possibilities of what could come. He would have had the complex sensory nervous system. Touch— he would have been able to feel the water rush by him. He would have floated alone in the ocean, deep enough that he'd have been covered in a world that knew only darkness and water, a womb for all of creation.

Could he have understood that he was the first?

Was it lonely or liberating, to be singularly alone like that?

Sometimes my partner urges me to just sit down. I am constantly in motion. I have learned that there is always more, that there is always something wrong and something to fix. Doing is a way to control. I no longer imagine floating in the middle of the ocean; I don't want to slow down or stop, because that means I have to be alone with myself. I work and go to school and go out to bars and parties and in all these things, I keep myself busy.

He reminds me: *Even god took a day of rest.*

It's funny because we don't believe in god, but I don't point that out. I tell him, *I have more work to do.* I worry that if I sit for too long, I will sink. It doesn't matter that I always feel like I'm on the verge of sinking anyways.

So I do more and more until it all comes crashing down. One day I wake up and realize I have nothing to do at all; I am suddenly unemployed and out of school for the summer. My only commitment for the day is to go to the beach with my partner.

I thought it might feel freeing if I was forced to stop—that it would feel like I was floating. Instead, I feel like thrashing, like fighting, unable to calm my body down long enough to come up for air. This, I know, is how people drown.

Two evolutionary scenarios of explanations as to why the comb jelly may be the first among all animals.

The first: The comb jelly may have evolved independently of other animals, not branching off the tree as much as splitting it in half, forging its path independently from the creatures to come.

The other explanation offers a theory: Perhaps the sponge evolved its simple form from the jelly's more complex one. Perhaps evolution is not a single straight line, with each generation becoming more complex than the last—maybe it's not just always having to do more.

Maybe it's simpler than all that.

In the beginning, there was only darkness. Then light. Then the waters.

Alex sits on the shore waiting for me. Lying in the ocean, I am alone.

I pull myself below the water and close my eyes, and my body feels weightless and alive, the way it did in the beginning.

To a Child
Who Does Not Yet Exist—

BY THE TIME you could be old enough to read this, it's likely that you already know something about bats. Perhaps you are afraid of them, believe them to be evil or malicious creatures the way they are sometimes portrayed in books and movies. Or maybe you, as I did as a child, find yourself drawn to them. Maybe you search for bats in all the dark places you find—basements, woodsheds, caves that answer only in echoes when you call for the friends you hope to make.

Did you know bats are born into an act of trust? Typically the smaller an animal is, the less time they spend pregnant. But despite only weighing around seventy grams, bats are pregnant for nearly as long as humans. For seven long months they hold their children inside themselves, allow their bodies to grow large and swollen with life. Seven, as you may know, is a number of completeness and perfection. So at the end of the seventh month, mother bats give birth upside down to one, single child who is up to a third of their own weight.

Because they are born upside down, the first thing that a baby bat does is fall. Eyes stuck together, completely blind, they drop down to the world below before they have the chance to open their mouths to scream. The mother must move quickly; in one motion she must offer her child up to the world and open her wings to catch it, protect it from earthly laws to which we are all bound. When this moment—this original trust exercise—is over, she then holds her newborn close to her body. It is a silent promise of safety that she will not let go without warning again.

I have never been needed like that before, the way a baby needs so completely.

I have been considering your maybe-future-existence today. Getting to a place where the possible-you is actually possible has not been easy. Right now, you, like the bat, exist in a liminal space, between this world and another, in maybe a hundred of the thousands of possible futures that lie before me. I am at a crossroads in life now; I am just starting to make true and tough decisions about the future. Do I want to get married? Do I want to live in a city, or move home to the rural landscape of the mountains, or something in between? Do I want children? These questions become more urgent each day, and perhaps because of that, I have been thinking about the possible-you more often.

There is a reason people hate bats; they cannot understand the place they have in this world, cannot see the goodness of the creature through the darkness that surrounds them. I have been in dark places in my life, hidden in caves so deep that there was no light, tried to bury myself under the cover of night. I was once so sad I thought it would kill me. It was during one of those times that the almost-you, the *possibility* of you, felt real.

You were not wanted. You were feared. I wasn't ready.

I had woken up on a mattress I didn't know with a man I had never met before, my thighs stained red and ugly. I didn't understand then, the wreckage that had been done to my body. But I knew you represented a death, the end of life as I knew it, if you could call the barely surviving that I was doing a kind of living. For seven days, I bent over the edge of my bed and prayed that you had not created your own genesis story in the darkness of my womb, that you had not mistaken the broken rubble of my body for a cave of comforts, for a home you could live in.

I drank three glasses of water before bed on the seventh night and slept with my arms wrapped tightly around my stomach, as if I could press you back into non-existence. The next morning I squatted over a pregnancy test that, after a moment of panicked waiting, offered me a single stripe, crossing you out of the world before you could enter it. I felt relief, of course, but the possible-you had been born inside my mind, and you have lived and grown there ever since.

I am older now, old enough to tell you that should you come to exist, it is because I want you. I am at a place now where having a child does not feel like a death. Instead, it is simply a transformation of life. The lives where you exist and the ones where you don't no longer seem at odds with each other—they are just two different paths that only I can see, only I can choose. Either way, the future that you would come into is one where you have been chosen.

I worry, of course. How could I not? I worry about the possibility of dropping you in a hundred different ways; that I will be a bad mother and leave terrible, unfixable scars across your psyche by virtue of my existence; that you may inherit the great sadness that has tried to consume me from the inside out; that you will have to leave me. The last one is inevitable. Even bats, who know that their mothers demonstrably saved them, still fly away sometime.

I try to imagine you, the way you would exist in this world; maybe you will be born completely bald, like I was. My mother, your grandmother, says that when I first came into this world she was convinced I was not her child; *her eyes are so big,* she said, words slurred from the pain medicine. I imagine you something like that, with large eyes, ready to experience all the wonders life has to offer.

The possibility of it all is so much that my heart feels ready to break out of my chest just thinking about it.

Sometimes my boyfriend and I talk about children. He's currently in the running for the person most likely to be your father, certainly, but it is hard for me actually to consider the other half of the equation that would make you because in my imagination, you are so fully and completely mine.

In the country Tonga, the bat is considered sacred, the physical manifestation of a separable soul. I know that should you become a reality, you will take a piece of me with you—a fragment of my soul snapped off and embedded into yours, so that you will always carry the innate, primal knowledge that I am learning to live, with my arms spread wide, ready to catch you should you fall.

THE MEANING OF SPARROWS

A WOMAN has a dream like a fairy tale.

The dream begins like this: there is a man, a Bluebeard figure, who turns his wives into birds. Sparrows, specifically, with small, thin bodies and fragile bones that could snap under the weight of a punch. In the dream, the woman knows—the way you half remember a movie you watched as a child—that all three wives will escape, but only the last wife will live. In the same dream—because this is the logic of the worlds of unawakened people—the woman is also the second wife.

The woman wakes up from the dream to go to work teaching composition to eighteen-year-olds with hopes the size of hot air balloons, kids that still believe the world can be what they make it. She is jealous of them for this sometimes. She likes her job but wants dental benefits because half her mouth has been hurting since June, and she can feel the rot coming from her tooth dripping like mud leaking down a mountainside.

She cannot afford to go get it checked out, cannot stand the idea of being told she has another cavity. The woman has so many cavities that she has sometimes convinced herself she can taste the metal when she eats certain foods. The woman is always in a dull state of pain and cradles her cheek in her hand the same way she might carry a soft fruit. The woman has recently begun drinking at night again, most nights again, to help with the ache of it all.

The woman is depressed and anxious, and her eating disorder has been flaring up. Well, her thoughts of disordered eating, which is what she calls it. After work, she stands in front of the mirror and cups her falling breasts, her stomach, her thighs. She considers killing herself in a passive, thoughtless sort of way. There is just so much of her. Where did it all come from? It seems like she fell asleep one night in a certain life and woke up this morning in another.

She tries to tell herself that this is healing too. Her body has endured so much—the abuse at her hands and others'. Sometimes getting better just means better than then, not the best she'll ever be.

She smiles at herself in the mirror the way the mental health Instagram influencers have told her will help. She thinks about how ugly and crooked her teeth are. She wonders if all celebrities really have dentures. She wonders if she could get dentures. She wonders if dentures would look nice at her funeral. She drinks.

The woman doesn't sleep well that night, or most nights, possibly because of the drinking. On the nights she does sleep, she wakes up at 2 a.m. like clockwork, sweaty and nervous as if she has recently escaped something.

Her partner lies in bed and snores. Sometimes she cries at night and sometimes he comforts her; sometimes she cries and sometimes he rolls over. She wants to get married one day, and he says *sure*. She apologizes for being all need and no give, and he claims *it's fine,* but she doesn't believe him.

She believes, in the back of her mind, that he may love another—or at least, that he may confide in another about how terrible she is, how ridiculous her crying seems, how she is always taking and never able to give as much back. She hears him talk in low tones on the phone in other rooms, sees questionable texts come up on his phone when they are out in public. She cries more, over silly things like her own thoughts, and he sighs again.

She tells herself again that this is healing too—that should he leave, she will be fine. Though the idea of it hurts in an aching, lovesick way, it is no longer enough to make her fall completely to pieces. It has been so much worse before.

When she finally falls asleep, she is holding her mouth in her hand.

The next day she wakes up and her back is stiff and pricked, as if feathers had been pulled from her one by one. She tries to work but is distracted.

It's the dream.

The wives meant to die.

She cannot stop thinking about them.

When she is supposed to be grading papers, she instead searches the internet for clues. She learns sparrows are thought to carry ancestral knowledge, and this information feels right, like something she had known before and forgot. Which ancestors are speaking to her?

Another website says sparrows represent the souls of the dead. But how can that be right, when the sparrow of her dream is only about to die? Or is it her own thoughts of death, bored of haunting her during the day so they crept into the night?

All day, she does this, researching until she feels numb other than the pain falling from her mouth, worse than before. When she looks in the mirror, she sees only the bags under her eyes swelled, her shoulders hunched forward in a state of protection. That night she sleeps, but just barely.

She tries to forget about it all. It means nothing. Dreams are just that: figments, an imagination gone wild, the brain trying to make narrative of shapes and sounds.

So why does she still feel tethered to it?

Why does she sense her own death around every corner?

Why is it that she keeps imagining dead women and birds inside the closets of her bedroom?

She opens the closet door idly, just for something to do. When she blinks the dead women and birds are gone, but she knows she saw them, just knows it. She wonders if she's already dead or just sleep-deprived.

She doesn't tell her partner; he would tell her she was silly—or worse, would tell someone else she was crazy. She carries her vulnerability in her pockets, close to her hips. She cannot afford to be put away; health insurance won't cover it. She tells herself healing is just being better than she used to be, not the best every day. She wonders if this is a backslide. She spends all day imagining she is still asleep, taking a nap mid-morning, in the afternoon, and again that evening. She falls behind on work but doesn't care about catching up. What does work matter if this is all a dream?

In the night, the man and the birds return to her again and she is one of them, a woman meant to die. They are flying, they are running, they are afraid. What are they afraid of? What is she afraid of? The world is brown and dusty like the desert she has never been to. Her little bird heart is beating fast. How do you escape a man like this? How do you escape your life? How do you escape your death? The woman who is not the woman, but a bird wife, knows the first is dead. She knows that she is next the same way a knitter knows they weave misfortune into their lover's sweater. She walks through a house, a grand house with beautiful high ceilings and long windows. She can feel herself being stalked. She is so small, and every shadow threatens to devour her. She can sense movement out of the corner of her eye, but when she turns to look, there is nothing there. Where is he? Why can't she fly anymore? Everything is getting darker. Why is she opening the closet doors when she knows what waits for her inside—has seen the bones like her, the empty eyes, the blood so red it is almost black? Why is everything getting darker?

The woman wakes up in a sweat to the sounds of birds outside her windows.

She wants to cry but does not. Instead, she gets up and makes herself coffee. Her partner sleeps in the next room, and she can hear his phone buzz with the words of another, someone who she suspects does not dream in unclear fables and death. She wonders if it is too early to open a bottle of wine. Her fingers hover over the bottle, slick and shiny and red. It would be so easy to pour it into a travel mug.

She used to be so good at drinking in secret, in the mornings. She could do it again. She could give in and be so much worse than she is. The temptation is there. It would be so much easier than fighting what feels like an often-uphill battle to being better.

She leaves it behind and puts on a green dress, the one her partner bought her last month. She steps outside. She drinks her water. Above her, the birds wake up to face another day.

STEPS TO MAKING THE PERFECT CUP OF BLACK COFFEE

1. Become Too Poor for Creamer

This is, of course, what will force you to learn to make a good cup of black coffee. It will start with simply forgetting, blowing past the vanilla fat-free creamer without thinking. Eventually, you will walk by the creamers of all kinds with sad eyes, having already calculated exactly how much money can be spent at the store, the exact price of every item in the cart, and knowing that creamer did not make the cut.

2. Move In with a Man Who Takes Coffee Seriously

After combining households, together you will own two French presses, a cold brew pitcher, one red single-server pour-over that sits atop the cups and *drip drip d r i p s* so slowly it makes your fingers shake, a grinder for whole beans, and the Ninja coffee maker with three settings that a sorority sister gave you nearly five years ago now. One setting doesn't work, but it is still one of the nicest and most expensive things you own, and it is the only thing you both use now.

3. Buy Coffee Beans

Not espresso beans, because you'll be jittery for days straight when you insist on drinking the espresso as full cups because you paid for them, *damn it, and we'll use them.*

4. Grind the Beans

It is loud, ugly, and lacks ritual, but it must be done. The beans smell like morning, and you must scoop them into the body of the grinder. The lid presses into the body to force the metal blades to cut everything up. When you flip it over to release the lids and grounds, you must be careful. Ground coffee scatters across the small counter you keep these tools on, brown dust your boyfriend never cleans up even though he's the one who keeps missing the careful flip of the lid.

5. Fill the Water Holder

Use the cup that will eventually hold the coffee to cut down on dishes. Pour in two cups of coffee if you're feeling frisky and think you might have a second coffee later.

6. Replace the Filter

The filter from yesterday will still be in the machine and wet, so you must dump it into the trash. Try not to touch it. Put a fresh one in and then two scoops of ground coffee in the cone it creates.

7. Press "Rich Brew" Because the Regular Brew Button Is Broken

It's fine. Rich brew does the job fine.

8. Go Do Something Else

Or many somethings. Walk the dog. Answer student emails. Grade papers.

Argue with your boyfriend about if clothes on the floor should still be considered clean. Stare at the unwashed dishes without doing them. Stare at the unmade bed without making it. Feel yourself being unmade and undone. Think about the gray hair that you found in the shower. Think about how your dog prefers your boyfriend. Think about how coffee used to be: a silent ritual to be done in the early light of a clean kitchen because it was only yours—the whole world might have been yours then—and the dog would sit next to you and the French press would move ever so slowly through the water, and you would use just a little bit of creamer and it was perfect.

9. Know the Coffee Is Done

You will have long stopped hearing the beep announcing the cup full. It's too hot for you then anyways. This is a sense you cannot explain or teach, cannot set your clock to it or prepare in any way. It comes from the back of your chest, behind your lungs. You will be in the middle of something else entirely and then—the coffee is done. You simply know it to be true.

10. Take the First Sip

Your boyfriend will be in the kitchen involved in his own coffee-making process. There will be a cup in each hand, full of water and instant coffee he insists is *really good actually* and pours one into the other and the other into the one and over and over again until the alchemy is just so.

His hair will be dark and his eyes will be green, and he will be wearing a sweatshirt you got him for his birthday two years ago. Though it is almost lunch, he will have just made breakfast by then, and it will smell like bacon and bagels and the jam you like. He will smile at you.

How is your coffee? he will ask as you take a sip.

Despite the dishes, despite the work waiting for you, despite the missing creamer, despite the growing pains of life, you will smile back at him and tell the truth. *It's perfect.*

AND IT WAS GOOD

H E LAYS ME DOWN in the afternoon, during his lunch break, on the couch. The sunlight makes our eyes bright and bodies warm, and we are drawn together like the leaves are drawn to the ground around this time of year. Our living room is full from where our two apartments have recently combined into one. Every wall has furniture pressed to the edges, with only half of the long French doors free to open, free to lead us to our balcony where the southern heat makes every day hazy and heavy no matter the season.

We do it on my couch, not his, because we are long but it's longer. The afternoons are longest. Outside, his tomato plant bears its first flower. Inside, butter melts in my coffee because we don't have any creamer. My nails dig homes into his skin. His hands dig into my side, but I do not notice until I find small bruises the size of blueberries, of his fingerprint, later.

After, I stand up and I break a glass full of water. I hit it with my foot and watch it tumble off the coffee table and smash against the hardwood floor like a punch. It shatters across the floor in tiny pieces, making the wooden strips sparkle like I had tossed diamonds into dirt.

I expect him to be mad. I expect men to be mad at me, usually.

I have known the taste of blood, the sound of teeth rattling in my skull;

I have known when pain is meant to be cruel, and my body has learned to be ready for it.

But he is not angry.

In fact, he is very rarely angry, as even-tempered and dependable as the daily rain that knocks on our windows; he gets a broom, picks up the shards, makes everything clean for me again. Then he takes me to the bedroom and does it all again. The rain kisses glass. A bird calls for its lover. He bites my neck. When I tell him I'm about to cum he says *good, good, good.*

Three days later, I'm going into the grocery store, and I find a shard of glass he missed buried in my sole. Through the pain, I find myself smiling.

To Outline the Moon

Full Moon

I have a hundred memories that all feel like falling asleep. There is the smell of logs burning in a firepit and the taste of burnt marshmallow on my tongue and the sounds of men's voices talking and laughing. At the time, almost every man I know is a father or an uncle, and everywhere I look there are mountains.

As a child, still genderless with youth, family members teach me the language that nature speaks, show me how to follow moss and recognize bird songs and make fists out of rope. I learn to lay my body down against a canoe and trust the river to rock me back and forth as if I am still buried in the depths of my mother. On long trips down river, we dock our boats on muddy shores. When I stand in the shallow water, I squint looking for the tadpoles that live just above the sand, watching them swim around in circles. We climb up rocks and jump, sinking lower and lower and lower into the water until it becomes so dark I can't see.

Before there are apps that can outline constellations, my father does it with his hand. We sit side by side in grass turning wet by the night, and he points out the triangles and circles that hold stories in their imaginary lines. He teaches me about men that became legends, achieving immortality through their place in the sky. The moon hangs center, bright and swollen full. He asks me to consider the impossible: What would it be like to walk the hills of space?

My father is a big man. His laugh fills a room. He holds court among his friends offering sweeping, open gestures with one hand, cradling a home-brewed beer with the other, and gives practiced tellings of a personal history that I can recite like a myth. He is the youngest of nine children, the products of a teacher and a preacher. He goes camping with his brothers once or twice a year, for weeks at a time. He only has daughters. He loves looking up. Once, he woke me and my sisters up at midnight, moving quietly between our rooms. "There's a meteor shower," he says. "Come with me."

We drive to a field nearby, and we lie on the grass where the county fair will be held later in the summer and watch the balls made of dust and ice trail across the sky. We stay out there for three hours before we go home again. When I wake up again, it feels like it had all been a dream.

Waning Gibbous

I once thought I saw a blood moon, but it was only the reflection of a pit fire.

It looks down at me during an early July night, while firefighters run for their gear, shove their masks down, tighten their gloves. I must be at least a hundred yards from the flames, but the heat still threatens to lick me clean. The men go to help hold the hose that attempts to extinguish the flame, which is bright and wild and could, without question, eat us to the bone.

It won't, of course. The whole scene is playing a trick on our senses. I'm spending a week of my summer working to help train firefighters at camp, a job I have no qualifications for except for my knack for ropes and love of poker. The flame is carefully contained to a hole in the earth that we helped dig earlier in the week. The firefighters are only practicing putting out a large flame together, and I am there to hold glasses and cell phones as they take turns going in to kill the pit fire.

I take a picture to show my dad later; he had worked a similar summer gig as a teen and was the one who encouraged me to apply. We mostly fight, my dad and I, and my mother says this is because we are too similar, not because of the actual content of the argument.

We're like a trick coin with two heads, both headstrong and angry people. We even look alike; our baby pictures get confused for one another. We don't really know how to say I love you, but sometimes we sit together in his truck, a rust-colored Ford older than I am, with the windows down and sing Hank Williams songs, and that feels close enough to saying it that I don't think either of us minds.

The fire goes out, and the heat disappears alongside it. It gets relit in the pit again so a new group can run in, a circular dance of light and loss. The empty part of the moon could be just a sliver of a smile.

Last Quarter

My dad and my Uncle Jim taught me how to shuffle cards and play poker. My Uncle Jim taught me a lot of things, I know that, but what I remember is him sitting across from me at the picnic table, our pennies rusted dark, the crickets loud. We are set up somewhere deep in the Monongahela National Forest, and a bug zapper lights our faces as sunset, bleeding red, fades to black. He plays many roles: he is an uncle, a son that mows my grandfather's grass every week, a sibling to eight others, a father to my cousins, and my middle school principal. I always wave to him in the halls, and I can never skip school.

My dad gives me ten dollars in pennies with the promise that I split my winnings with him. Other players—cousins, aunts, more uncles—join the game just to leave again. The moon is cut as clean as a deck of cards. I practice his stance, my elbows up on the red-checkered plastic tablecloth that covers the picnic table, my eyes moving to follow his. The plains of my uncle's face hold his mouth in a permanent look of seriousness. I tilt the corners of my lips down to become his other half in hopes of being taken as an equally serious player.

What we talked about has been lost to time, but we played into the night and I walked away with thirty dollars in change, fifteen after I gave my dad his cut. The constellations above us became clear as we sat around a fire, and I listened to my father and Uncle Jim laugh and speak in a language of intimacy, talking about memories and plans. They figured out the logistics for their back-country Canada trip. They told me about their hometown, which is also my hometown, and the changes it's made and the ways it's stayed the same. They talked about the hikes we did that day and the bike rides we'll all take together tomorrow.

When I got up to go to bed, they were still talking, and their voices became one sound.

Waning Crescent

I feel like the tadpoles I once watched swim in circles—around and around and around—trying to understand my father. He sells the truck. I move a few states away to flatter land. We do not fight anymore because we don't talk much at all. Not on purpose, just as part of never really talking to begin with. The distance makes me all the more interested in trying to understand who he is, and how that informs who I am.

As an adult I call to tell him that I'm going to the Grand Canyon next summer, and he tells me it's the trip he always wanted to take but never did. I feel him take over; he'll send me a tent, the same one I camped in with him growing up. He'll do some research for me. He'll make me a camp box if I let him know the dimensions of the back of my car.

"You won't believe the stars out there. And the moon!" he says. "It's gonna be hot. Do you have a good sleeping bag? You're going to have to start hiking again, if you can find any places to do it down there."

I welcome his intrusion, the shadow he casts. It is the only way I know how to feel close to him.

New Moon

There are nine phases of the moon. The new moon is the zero, a phase marked by nothing, a dark placeholder for where the light will be. No one breaks out their telescopes or looks up in awe at the empty space.

The first time I remember my father crying was just after our family dog passed. The second time is when he calls me to tell me Uncle Jim has died.

"It was so fast," he says to me. Five days between the diagnosis and death. As quick as a lifetime. I say nothing back because my mouth is nothing but a black hole, a gaping space where sound becomes lost.

They'll fly me back to say goodbye, he tells me. There won't be a casket. They're going to spread the dust of him back into the earth, so he can rest in the wilderness forever.

He and his siblings help prepare the memorial for their brother. The slideshow clicks through pictures. One shows all nine children standing together on the stairs of their parents' house. Jim stands with a half smile in the shadow of a tree. He is the one dark spot compared to his eight siblings, who stand in varying degrees of light.

Waxing Crescent

I know that the grief will live inside me for the rest of time, the same way I survive with a small rock in my knee and a silver scar across my knuckle, markers of a life spent outside. I inhabit a body intent on living.

I go home to the river, and I lie down in my canoe and let it rock me and wonder what it would feel like to flip, to sink so low into the water I can't see.

My father tries to learn to talk about Jim in past tense.

My chest feels like it carries a weight hanging between my lungs.

I dream I get a tattoo of the phases of the moon across my ring finger. It ends at the waxing crescent.

First Quarter

In October, my boyfriend and I go to a wedding in his hometown, in the backyard of a beach house. Everything is white: the house, the lights, the wine, the sky covered in clouds threatening to bathe us all in what I imagine would be salt water from the ocean. The ceremony takes less than ten minutes, and we spend the next hours dancing and laughing at memories I don't have, and after everyone else leaves, we go to the roof to watch the Atlantic at work.

The moon blends into the stars that blend into the light bouncing back off the sea. We toast to the past that made us and the future that we will become. That night I dream of falling asleep in the ocean.

The next morning I call my parents, and my father tells me about hiking up to deer camp to spread my uncle's ashes.

"It's one day at a time," he says.

Waxing Gibbous

In the middle of winter, I track through mud that holds onto my footprint. For a moment I realize I could die this way; one misstep and it could be a broken ankle or worse, no one would find me until I'm half-frozen, and why did I forget to put on gloves?

The air is crisp in the way it only is in the mountains, and the moon isn't quite full, but it's enough. There's a meteor shower tonight. The trees are honest and bare in its light, and I follow the moss to the river, where there will be a clearing. I can feel my heartbeat under the coat I borrowed from my father. The walk isn't long, and I can hear the waterfall.

I'm not going for any particular reason other than to try and count stars as they run their way across the sky. I am visiting from the city, and I want to be in the nature I grew up in as much as possible. When I finally reach the waterfall, I know without touch that it's cold, but my body wants to dive into it anyways. I dip one finger in, and the shock of almost ice against my skin is enough.

Full Moon

I know I will never completely understand my father, but we both have a hundred memories that all feel like falling asleep, and that is enough.

Months after Jim dies, my father and I find ourselves talking intently about a time in my childhood when he took me camping up and down the east coast for a summer. He says it was his brothers who taught him the secrets of nature, what wood burns best and how to tie bags of food to where bears couldn't get it. They showed him how to stand, a foot on each gunnel, and balance on a canoe's edges. He says before there were apps that could outline constellations, Jim would do it with one hand.

It's easy to imagine them driving to the same field my father took me to, where maybe they listened to Hank Williams and parked on the grass where the county fair would be held later in the summer. Maybe together, they discussed the men who became legends through their place in the night; maybe they rested against the dirt of the earth, watching balls made of dust and ice trail across the sky.

Scorpius

Lesath

When the earth was still new but human hubris already old, the hunter Orion claimed that he would kill every animal in the world, hunt down each creature until he had eradicated all but mankind. He told this to the goddess of the hunt, Artemis—perhaps he thought she would be impressed by his boasts. Perhaps she was, thinking him joking; for if he killed every animal on earth, what would there be left to hunt?

But no matter that. Gaia, Mother Earth herself, heard them, and knew that there was a kernel of true desire to his statement. So she crafted the scorpion in her hand, gave it claws and a tail laced with poison. She sent it to Orion, and he laughed—a creature so small! It could be crushed with his foot! And yet the scorpion killed Orion, struck him dead, his tail diving into Orion's simple human flesh, turning his blood into poison.

Artemis asked Zeus to place Orion in the stars so that he could be immortalized. He obliged, and Gaia demanded that the scorpion, the victor, join him. Now, every winter Orion can be seen hunting across the sky—but as the spring comes, he is chased away as the constellation Scorpius rises.

Shaula

For almost all of time, humankind has been obsessed with making shapes from stars. It is one of our singular, overall fixations. It makes sense; the heavens and animals they created from it offered stories about themselves, about human nature, a mirror for them to project their own myths on.

Ursa Major and Ursa Minor, mother and son, turned to bears for the rest of time.

Orpheus, made a swan, his lyre by his side, who couldn't help but look back.

Draco, who guarded the golden apples, dead by Hercules because even dragons die. There's something endearing about this, that we were able to look up and find ourselves.

κ-Sco

My birthday wasn't actually meant to be mine; born making a fist, it was as if I had stolen something and wouldn't let go. When my mother went into what would be her final ultrasound with me, my heartbeat was weaker than it should have been, and the doctors were concerned that I wouldn't make it to the due date. So I was born under the sign of Scorpio, brought screaming into the world in mid-November, underweight, my parents' first child.

ι¹-Sco

Prehistoric fossils show that scorpions have not changed their shape in a millennium. Incredibly resilient, they are in many ways indestructible. When there is not enough food, they are able to live for a year without it. Because they have book lungs, which are shaped like a shell cracked in half, they can last underwater for two days and survive. Once, researchers froze scorpions overnight, let them collect ice across their bodies, become as solid as gemstones. The next day, the scientists left their experiments in the sun to thaw, only to watch the scorpions raise themselves from the dead and walk away, unbothered by the whole affair.

Scorpio is a fixed sign, famous for resistance to change, great willpower, and inflexibility. When I tell my mother this, she says she's not surprised; she remembers when I was three and she had to carry me, screaming and crying, out of a grocery store. I had wanted something, and she wouldn't give it to me; it was a typical childhood tantrum.

I put you in the car seat, my mother (a Cancer) tells me, *and then you had the audacity to demand an apology from me!*

Sargas

Wouldn't it be nice if that was all true?

The idea of predestination, I mean, coincidence being truth, being able to blame parts of me on only the stars—the parts that are mean, that are violent, that are intense and cruel. Scorpios are famously one of the most sexual signs, and I realized recently that I have only ever been in relationships with other Scorpios. I have found them in bar bathrooms, at parties, felt the heat of their bodies across crowded rooms. We always find each other. We often want to hurt each other. It could be fate.

η-Sco

I'll admit it: I'm prone to the romantic notions of fate, the idea of finding meaning in random actions. I like coincidences, is what I'm saying.

Was Orion always going to die from the scorpion's sting? Was it written in the stars before he became made of stars himself? Was it just cosmic coincidence that Gaia overheard them? Are the stars simply stars, only meaningful in the ways we look at them, the stories we find shining inside them?

Maybe it is, in some ways, easier to believe that I was always meant to be damaged like I was. It certainly makes it easier to avoid circling around the what-I-should-have-dones, the alternate routes I could have chosen in life to avoid the pain. If I was always meant to be in pain, then this pain is not my fault.

ζ²-Sco

Life has been some combination of fairy-tale coincidence and joie de vivre and shocks of beauty together with some hurtful self-questioning.

—Sylvia Plath, Scorpio

μ¹-Sco

Coincidences are inevitable and are actually less remarkable than we think them to be—or at least that's what the scientists say.

Carl Jung (a Leo) had a theory of synchronicity, where one can assume that events may be connected by causality, but they may also be connected by meaning; essentially, the experiences of events are causally unrelated, and yet their occurrence together, the existence they share in space, has meaning for the person who notices them.

ε-Sco

Scorpions have eight legs. Scorpio is the eighth sign of the zodiac calendar. Scorpius has eight especially distinctive, bright stars, including Antares (α Sco), known as the rival of Mars for its red color. Mars is one of the ruling planets for Scorpio. In the Middle Ages, eight was the number of "unmoving" stars in the sky and therefore meant perfection of planetary energy; eight is the only positive Fibonacci number—other than one—considered a perfect cube. Buddha's principal teaching involves eight noble truths; in Islam, there are eight gates to heaven. Flipped on its side, the number eight is infinity itself. In the Bible, eight is representative of creation, new beginnings, and the resurrection; the sign of Scorpio is representative of rebirth. Eight is part of creation, the allowance of survival; it is the atomic number of oxygen.

Funnily enough, before I knew any of this, I considered my lucky number to be eight.

τ-Sco

My partner now is incredibly stubborn like me, fixed in his ways, the first child to his parents, born early and severely underweight, and of course, a Scorpio too. He has bright eyes, like two stars shining from under his dark curly hair. When we find ourselves in the night, we are drawn together, as if the gods designed it this way. We were born four years and four days apart.

What a coincidence, right?

Antares

Just coincidence. Dots. Connections.

Dschubba

The meaning might just be for me alone, which is fine too. Not everyone is interested in stargazing. It's the same kind of questioning: Am I prone to drawing the lines in between because I am a romantic? Or am I a romantic first and because of that, I have learned to draw lines between connections? Either of these things could be true. Maybe both of them are, and they just exist in different spaces on the same plane.

Acrab

Do I contradict myself? Very well then, I contradict myself.
—Walt Whitman, Gemini (of course.)

The quote is famous on its own, but it comes from the poem *Song of Myself*, which has another one of my favorite lines: *I believe a leaf of grass is no less than the journey-work of the stars.* For of course, the two are created from the same iron and rust and stardust.

We're all made of the same cosmic material, from me to Orion.

v-Sco

When the earth was old and human hubris older—long after the hunter Orion claimed that he would kill every animal in the world, hunt down each creature until he had eradicated all but mankind—I stood under the night sky and looked up and watched him look back. The scorpion was on the other side of the earth, waiting to attack.

I imagine myself as the scorpion diving its tail into human flesh.

I imagine myself as Orion, watching the blood bloom red.

The two will never be seen in the night sky at the same time, but they both are in the sky all the same.

The constellations, resurrections of the dead, rise, and I look for myself—somehow, still alive—reflected back in them.

Acknowledgments

The following essays have been published elsewhere,
often in altered forms:

"What I Remember," *trampset*

"Did Dolphins Cry," *(mac)ro(mic)*

"An Incredibly Brief and Unfinished History of Sound,"
    Hippocampus Magazine

"How the Cicada Screams," *The Threepenny Review*

"Once, I Saw a Monarch Butterfly Dead on the Pavement,"
    Lammergeier Magazine

"To Survive Hypothermia, You Must Ignore Everything Your Body
    Tells You," *Meeting Gods in Basement Bars and Other Ways to
    Find Forgiveness* (Ethel)

"Forgotten Synonyms for Grief," *Barren Magazine*

"Becoming Fireflies," *Rejection Letters*

"Bar Bathroom Graffiti in New Orleans: A One Year Catalog,"
    Hippocampus Magazine

"First, there was the Comb Jelly," *Epoch Press*

"To a Child Who Does Not Yet Exist," *Futures Anthology*

"To Outline the Moon," *Alaska Quarterly Review*

As is the case with most books, there are more influences on this book than there are pages inside it. As I must limit myself, I want to say generally thank you to everyone involved and supportive of this work and all my other ideas, concepts, and stories.

First, thank you to my family, especially my parents. Thank you for teaching me to release the turtles we found in the backyard. Thank you for not hiding the deaths of bugs in the basement. Thank you to my father for showing me how to chop wood and balance on the gunnels of a canoe. Thank you to my mother, who would let me sit on the edge of the ocean's surf and watch fiddler crabs for hours. Thank you both for giving me the incredible gift of books.

Thank you to my professors at West Virginia Wesleyan College, including Dr. Katherine Antolini, Dr. Jess Scott, Jessie Van Eerden, Doug Van Gundy, and Dr. Ashley Lawson, as well as my thesis committee at the University of New Orleans: Richard Goodman, Randy Bates, and Dr. David Rutledge.

Thank you to my beautiful UNO cohort, Leah Myers and Teo Chesney, along with my enduring workshop group, including Ellis Anderson, Reda Wigle, and Amie Geistman. Without your insights both in workshop and at the bar after, this would just be a pile of essays. It is only with your help and guidance that it has become a book.

Thank you to Kati Baker, Nancy Isner, Jessie Kelly, Marissa Gain, Zoë Higgins, Jack Cape, Alex Tronson, C.A. Munn, Oliva Cape, Jessica Brasseur, Skye Jackson, Michelle Nicholson, Nikki Ummel, Kimberly Wolf, and a million other writers and creators and friends who served as witnesses to this process.

Thank you to the Belle Point Press team, Michael and Casie Dodd, for believing in, editing, and making this book real. It's an honor to be part of this press.

Thank you to Elizabeth Clever, who survived it all with me.

Thank you always to Alex Galbraith, for everything and more.

KIRSTEN RENEAU is a writer living in the South. She graduated from West Virginia Wesleyan College and received an MFA from the University of New Orleans. She is the author of two chapbooks, and her work has been published in *The Threepenny Review, Alaska Quarterly Review, Reed Magazine,* and others. This is her first full-length essay collection.

Belle Point Press is a literary small press
along the Arkansas-Oklahoma border.
Our mission is simple: Stick around and read.
Learn more at bellepointpress.com.